ABIDING WORD

ABIDING WORD

SUNDAY REFLECTIONS FOR YEAR A

Barbara E. Reid, OP

LITURGICAL PRESS
Collegeville, Minnesota

www.litpress.org

Library of Congress Cataloging-in-Publication Data

Reid, Barbara E.
  Abiding word : Sunday reflections for year A / Barbara E. Reid, OP.
    pages   cm
    ISBN 978-0-8146-3314-4 (alk. paper) — ISBN 978-0-8146-3474-5 (e-book)
    1. Church year meditations. 2. Bible—Meditations. 3. Catholic Church—Prayers and devotions. 4. Catholic Church. Lectionary for Mass (U.S.). Year A. I. Title.

BX2170.C55R425   2013
242'.3—dc23

                                                          2013013130

For my mother, Christine O'Brien Reid,

who has taught me and so many others

how to abide with the Word

in her eight decades of life.

Ad multos annos!

CONTENTS

PREFACE

At the beginning of the Fourth Gospel, John the Baptist watches Jesus walk by and exclaims to two of his disciples, "Look, here is the Lamb of God!" (John 1:36, NRSV). The two disciples begin to follow Jesus. When he turns and sees them following, he asks, "What are you looking for?" They reply, "Rabbi, where are you staying?" to which Jesus responds, "Come and see." So they do, and they remain with him that day (John 1:36-39, NRSV). Staying, remaining, abiding (these are various ways that the Greek verb *menein* can be translated), is the primary response of a disciple. Different from the Synoptic Gospels, where disciples are more often seeking to understand who Jesus is, in the Fourth Gospel, the search is framed in terms of knowing where Jesus abides.

One of the key ways to abide in Jesus is through his word. Jesus tells those who believe in him, "If you continue in my word, you are truly my disciples, and you will know the truth, and the truth will make you free." Conversely, those who oppose him and look for an opportunity to kill him do so "because there is no place in you for my word" (John 8:31-38, NRSV).

Another mode of abiding with Jesus is through Eucharist. After he feeds the multitude, Jesus tells his followers, "Those who eat my flesh and drink my blood abide in me and I in them" (John 6:56, NRSV). This mutual indwelling, we in Christ and Christ in us, is deepened each Sunday through the word and at the table.

I offer this collection of reflections on the Scripture readings for each Sunday and solemnity for the Lectionary Year C as a weekly aid to enter more deeply into the abiding word, and to enable a renewed response to remain with Jesus. These reflections first appeared in *America* magazine, from November 22, 2010 to November 14, 2011 (vol. 203, no. 15–vol. 205, no. 15), and have been slightly edited for this volume.

I invite you to establish a pattern of dwelling with the word each day, if possible. Some suggestions for how to approach the word follow. Many find it helpful to set aside the same block of time each day, and to sit in one particular place, in a chapel, or in a favorite easy chair, claiming this as your sacred time and sacred space. Sit with your spine straight, feet flat on the floor, and concentrate on your breathing. As you breathe in, and breathe out, invite the Spirit, whom Jesus promised will abide with us always (John 14:17), to open your mind, eyes, ears, and heart to the word that the Holy One wants to give you this day. Consciously set aside all other concerns, distractions, and worries. Imagine leaving them outside the door of your holy space. If they try to intrude into your prayer, tell them they have to wait until you have finished, and that you will pick them up again later.

Open the Scriptures and read the text slowly and contemplatively. Savor each word and phrase. Imagine yourself as one of the characters in the story if the text is a narrative. What do you see? hear? smell? feel? Read through the text again slowly and prayerfully. Is there a particular word or phrase that catches your attention? Stay with that word or phrase and let it take deeper root in you. Wait patiently for whatever it is that is being revealed to you in that word. Even if there is no clear insight or special meaning that emerges, trust that the word is abiding in you and unleashing its transformative power in you. Let yourself be led to see differently, for example, from the perspective of those made poor, of women, or of those not like yourself. Set aside what you "know" the text means and let yourself be surprised by the Spirit. Respond with thanks for what has been given to you by the abiding One. Hold on to a word or phrase from the Scripture and return to it throughout the day. Jot it down in your prayer journal, so you can return to it at another time. Let its meaning continue to unfold as you abide in it and it in you.

In the Gospel of John, as Jesus approaches his death, he tells his disciples that he prepares a dwelling place for each one, so that where he is they may also be. Thomas struggles, insisting he does not know the way. Jesus assures him that Jesus himself is the way, the truth, and the life. The abiding place, then, is not a special "room with a view," so to speak, but is Jesus himself. Abiding in Jesus leads also to indwelling with the One who sent him and with the Spirit, as Jesus prayed for oneness, "I in them" and "they in us" and "I in them" and "you in me" (John 17:20-23).

The gift of abiding in Christ and Christ in the believer is a priceless treasure meant not only for oneself. It is a fruitful gift, one that is intended to be shared with others, producing a harvest of transformative love (John 15:1-8).

Barbara E. Reid, OP
Feast of the Presentation of the Lord, 2012

PREPARING TO WAGE PEACE

First Sunday of Advent

Readings: Isa 2:1-5; Ps 122:1-2, 3-4, 4-5, 6-7, 8-9;
Rom 13:11-14; Matt 24:37-44

*"They shall beat their swords into plowshares
and their spears into pruning hooks"* (Isa 2:4)

Ever since the attacks on the World Trade Center in New York on September 11, 2001, there have been nonstop warnings to be alert to possible terrorist attacks. In US airports repeated public announcements from Homeland Security advise whether the level of alert is yellow, orange, or red. People are asked to be aware and wary.

Today's second and third readings want us to move to red alert. Paul says it is time to wake from sleep. The gospel warns us to stay awake and not be caught unaware. The images of what happens to those who are unprepared sound frightening: a thief in the night breaks in; one man in a field is taken and the other one left; one woman grinding at the mill is taken and the other one left. "Be prepared," Jesus warns.

As we enter into Advent once again, we are not preparing for the coming of the Christ Child; that already happened more than two thousand years ago. Rather, in Advent, we break our normal routine and move into heightened alert to perceive more intensely the ways in which Emmanuel, God-with-us, is moving us toward that vision of peace and unity that Isaiah so eloquently describes in the first reading. The prophet dreams of how all people stream toward the city of peace, all dwell in unity, swords are beaten into plowshares, spears into pruning hooks, and there is no more training for war again.

In the second reading Paul gives concrete advice about how we might do this intense preparation for the coming fullness of the peaceable kingdom. Paul exhorts Christians to "throw off the works of darkness and put on the armor of light." He recognizes that the peace of which Isaiah dreamed, and which the coming of Christ brought about in a new way, does not come without a struggle. It takes more than just wishing and longing to make it a reality. He imagines Christians going into battle, metaphorically speaking.

To prepare for the struggle, Paul would have us polish up our body armor of virtues. He speaks of the kind of training one must undergo to be able to be the bearer of light. He warns against excesses and indulgences that make one sated and sluggish. Instead, traditional practices of prayer and fasting can hollow out inner space to tend the light we are asked to bear. Paul also warns against rivalry and jealousy. By putting on Christ, we don armaments of forgiveness and community building.

The readings for this Sunday urge us to go beyond defensive preparations. Readying ourselves for the full expression of the peaceable kingdom also entails initiating nonviolent action to dismantle weapons of war and transform whatever there may be in our hearts that is not yet able to wage peace. Swords are not beat into plowshares without intentional acts to dismantle the stockpile of weapons. The Second Vatican Council's Pastoral Constitution on the Church in the Modern World also reminds us, "As long as extravagant sums of money are poured into the development of new weapons, it is impossible to devote adequate aid in tackling the misery which prevails at the present day in the world" (Austin Flannery, *Vatican Council II: The Basic Sixteen Documents* [Northport, NY: Costello, 1996] 81).

The gospel today impresses upon us the urgency of engaging in the struggles for peace. The images of the unprepared ones whose homes are broken into or who are left behind are not meant to frighten us, but they remind us that there will be an end time when all our preparations, all our attempts to be alert, and all our efforts to disarm our hearts and wage peace will, in a critical moment, reach fruition. And we will be ready.

PRAYING WITH SCRIPTURE

1. How do you put on the armor of light?

2. What spiritual practices prepare you for the struggle to wage peace?

3. How does your faith community take actions to beat swords into plowshares?

BEARING GOOD FRUIT

Second Sunday of Advent

Readings: Isa 11:1-10; Ps 72:1-2, 7-8, 12-13, 17;
Rom 15:4-9; Matt 3:1-12

"Repent, for the kingdom of heaven is at hand!" (Matt 3:2)

"You can attract more flies with a teaspoon of sugar than with a barrel of vinegar," says a popular maxim. Yet in today's gospel, John the Baptist takes a very harsh approach. He is confrontational and uncompromising. There is nothing gentle or alluring about him. He demands repentance—urgently! And people flocked to him: "Jerusalem, all Judea, and the whole region around the Jordan were going out to him and were being baptized by him in the Jordan River as they acknowledged their sins." What did they find so attractive about John and his message?

One thing that could have had appeal was the desert locale where John was baptizing. There is a mysterious beauty to the desert where inner noise can be calmed and the senses are heightened, making one better able to discern priorities in the stark presence of the Holy One.

Another attractive characteristic of John was his wholehearted commitment to God's reign and the Coming One who would usher it in. When a person lives so completely and authentically what he or she proclaims, that witness is very compelling. Others are drawn not just to admire such a one, but to examine their own lives and to follow suit in whatever way possible. Although John's message at first seems off-putting, its effectiveness rested on the fact that it was not anger that fueled him, but a profound love of God and a passion to help everyone be ready for the imminent arrival of the One who is to come.

John had no patience, however, for those who were not sincere in their quest. It is startling that at the very first appearance in the gospel of the Pharisees and scribes, John slings insults at them, calling them a "brood of vipers." As the gospel progresses, we find that Pharisees and scribes are cast by Matthew as hypocrites and as those who lie in wait to trap Jesus, like snakes coiled to spring at any false move. John exposes their poisonous intent. If they were authentic seekers, that would be visible in their "good fruit."

What "good fruit" looks like is described by Isaiah in today's first reading. All creatures and the whole of creation exist in peaceful harmony. There is justice for all, especially for those most afflicted. Predators and prey dwell together in irenic oneness. Vulnerable little ones have no fear. Snakes like those John denounces no longer attack. In Isaiah's day it was thought that the new Davidic king, who would sprout from the stump of the conquered house of Jesse, would be the one to bring about this peaceable kingdom. John the Baptist points to Jesus as the one who brings it to fulfillment. Leaders alone, however, cannot by their faithfulness and wisdom establish the peaceable kingdom; their followers must also advance it.

There are serious and immediate consequences if the call to repentance is not heeded. John declares that any tree that does not produce fruit is cut down at the root and thrown into the fire. Such strong language is meant to get our attention. Like a mother who suddenly shouts out to keep her child from burning himself on a hot stove, a fiery prophet speaks in shocking ways to startle us into action. Today's readings invite us to find a desert spot where we can sink our roots deeply in contemplative oneness with the One who comes, extend our branches in welcome to those with whom we have been at odds, and let the Spirit pollinate us for an abundant harvest of fruitful goodness.

PRAYING WITH SCRIPTURE

1. Where is your "desert spot" where you can quiet your inner noise to listen to God?

2. How does your wholehearted commitment draw others to the Coming One?

3. What good fruit is ripening in you?

PATIENT EXPECTATION

Third Sunday of Advent

Readings: Isa 35:1-6a, 10; Ps 146:6-7, 8-9, 9-10;
Jas 5:7-10; Matt 11:2-11

*"Are you the one who is to come,
or should we look for another?"* (Matt 11:3)

There comes a time in most everyone's life when you wonder whether all the hard work and all the commitments are worth anything. Are you really making any difference in the world? Have you done with your life what you had hoped? Are you missing out on opportunities that may have passed by? That seems to be John the Baptist's frame of mind in today's gospel. He is in prison and his days are numbered. He had taken up a radical prophetic lifestyle, fasting, praying, calling people to repentance, preparing the way, and watching for the Coming One. Was he right?

John sends his disciples to ask Jesus, who points to all the signs that John's preaching was right on target. Through Jesus' ministry, to which John pointed, people who could not previously do so are now seeing, walking, and hearing. Many are healed and restored to life. Poor people are heartened with good news. All the soil so carefully tilled and tended by John is bearing the long-awaited fruit. Was he expecting something else? Jesus says to the crowds that John was "more than a prophet," and that there has been "none greater than John the Baptist." Presumably, this assurance is also conveyed to John, giving him heart to be able to quell the doubts and to endure patiently to the end.

Jesus then poses a forthright question to the crowds. Three times he asks why they went out to the desert and what they were expecting to see there. If they were looking for a prophet, not only have they seen the greatest of prophets, but they themselves are now called to exceed what John accomplished. How are the "least in the kingdom of heaven" supposed to surpass the greatest prophet? The readings today set forth attitudes that are essential for this.

The first reading invites us to be filled with joy and gladness, and to express this in singing and rejoicing, even when all seems desolate. The exiles had yet to see the concrete signs of restoration. Even before experiencing the anticipated healing and rebuilding, they were to enter into the ruined city singing for joy. This is not a naive refusal to see things as they are, but an expression of hope that springs from a deep conviction that God's saving deeds in the past will be manifest in the present and future as well, for those who have eyes to see. The very expectation that the parched wasteland will yield fragrant blooms begins to bring it into being.

While awaiting the fulfillment of our expectations and longings, the letter of James exhorts us to be patient. Using the example of a farmer, however, he makes it clear that patience does not mean sitting back and doing nothing. Like John the Baptist preparing the way for Jesus, a farmer meticulously tills the soil, clears away the rocks and weeds, and carefully plants the seed. It takes both the hard work of the farmer and the gift of rain, over which one has no control, to produce the anticipated harvest. Patience is doing everything one can, while at the same time relying utterly on the Divine Provider. The way to keep a firm heart in the waiting time, James says, is to refrain from complaining. Just as Jesus helped John's disciples to see the evidence of God's saving presence in their midst, so James urges us to look for the sprouts of hope that spring up even in the most parched desert. Expecting to see the desert bloom, or roses in December, as did Juan Diego, whom we remember on the feast of Our Lady of Guadalupe, we keep hope alive with patient endurance even in the midst of suffering and doubt.

PRAYING WITH SCRIPTURE

1. Ask Jesus to help you see the signs of his presence in the world around you.

2. Pray for the grace to be patient after doing all you can to prepare the way for Christ's full coming.

3. How does the message of Our Lady of Guadalupe to Juan Diego bring hope and healing?

OBEDIENCE OF FAITH

Fourth Sunday of Advent

Readings: Isa 7:10-14; Ps 24:1-2, 3-4, 5-6;
Rom 1:1-7; Matt 1:18-24

"When Joseph awoke,
he did as the angel of the Lord had commanded him" (Matt 1:24)

Today's teens are significantly more tolerant than their elders, according to a recent Pew Research Center study (*Millennials: A Portrait of Generation Next*, 2010). Young people born between 1981 and 2000 think nothing of dating members of other races. One student summed it up: "People are people, regardless of their skin color, religion, or culture. We have no reason to be fearful of anybody" (quoted in Ted Gregory, "Most Tolerant but Desensitized?," *Chicago Tribune* [November 13, 2010]). At the same time, studies of college students show that they are about 40 percent lower in empathy than students of the previous two or three decades (see the University of Michigan's Institute for Social Research).

Researchers suggested that the decrease in empathy is due to factors such as the numbing effects of violent video games, the impersonal nature of technology, and the glib, harsh language that is standard on television and online. Schools find that they need to construct activities designed to enhance understanding and empathy, which go far beyond tolerance.

Today's gospel brings to the fore the situation of Joseph, whose culture had little tolerance for a formally betrothed woman who was found to be with child by someone other than her intended. Joseph is a righteous man, faithful to all the demands of the Jewish law. The strictest interpretation of the law would call for the death of the apparently adulterous Mary (Deut 22:23-27). But Joseph is unwilling to denounce her publicly and searches for a way out. There cannot be a secret divorce; two witnesses are needed, and Mary's pregnancy cannot long be hidden.

Joseph's first solution is to avoid a public trial and divorce Mary quietly, without declaring the reasons (see Deut 24:1). This solution would preserve Joseph's reputation, but Mary would still be exposed to public shame. The only way to preserve Mary's honor would be for Joseph to complete his marriage to her and adopt the child as his own. In order for Joseph to make this choice, he has to shift focus away from concern about his own righteousness and reputation, and turn empathetically toward Mary. Only when he can make her the center of his attention, allowing himself to feel her distress, can he make the divinely directed choice that will uphold her honor at the price of his own.

In so doing, Joseph mirrors the divine action of empathy with humankind manifested in the incarnation. Just as the Holy One rectifies the broken relationship with humanity by becoming one with us, so Joseph rescues a dishonorable and potentially deadly situation by choosing to unite himself completely to Mary. Joseph exemplifies what their son Jesus will later teach his followers: one must go far beyond what the law requires in order to truly fulfill it.

This is what St. Paul calls "the obedience of faith" in his letter to the Romans. Obedience, as Paul elaborates later in this letter, is not blindly following commands, but comes from hearing, "and what is heard comes through the word of Christ" (Rom 10:17, NRSV). In fact, the word "obedience" (*hypakoē*) comes from the same root in Greek as does the verb "to hear" (*akouein*). In the gospel, Joseph's ability to hear with his heart the cries of his beloved Mary as well as the voice of our empathetic God leads to his faithful obedience. As Christmas approaches, it can be difficult for us to hear God's voice above the din of the many demands. When we pause each day to listen attentively, our faithful obedience, like that of Joseph, can have world-changing power as it creates the space for the Holy One to be ever birthed anew in our midst as God-with-us.

PRAYING WITH SCRIPTURE

1. Pray for an increase in empathy.

2. Ask God to lead you to the obedience of faith.

3. Give thanks for the ways in which you experience God-with-us.

LIGHT IN DARKNESS

The Nativity of the Lord

Readings: Isa 52:7-10; Ps 98:1, 2-3, 3-4, 5-6;
Heb 1:1-6; John 1:1-18

"[T]he light shines in the darkness,
and the darkness has not overcome it" (John 1:5)

Nearly the whole world was riveted by the rescue on October 14, 2010, of the thirty-three miners trapped for more than two months below the surface of the earth in Chile. Among the many concerns about how they would adjust to normal life again was the effect on their eyes of exposure to light after such a long time underground. The miners were given dark glasses to shield them from the sudden brightness. There had also been concern about the effect on their spirits from extended light deprivation. One of the miners, José Henríquez, took on the role of pastor to the group, leading them in prayer twice a day, so that they would not succumb to the darkness of despair. After their rescue, Henríquez spoke of what he considers his obligation to testify to how God used him to help bring his companions out of darkness into the light.

Today's gospel speaks of the Word becoming flesh as "light" that "shines in the darkness," and of its radiant effects. In the Fourth Gospel, darkness and light are frequently contrasted, with darkness serving as a metaphor to signify everything that is opposed to God. It should be noted that this literary convention is not intended to feed racism, privileging light skin over dark. In fact, Jesus and the people of his land would not have been pale-skinned. The evangelist often uses this dichotomy, light versus darkness, to set before the reader the choice between belief and unbelief.

The prologue makes three important assertions about the light. First, the light that was coming into the world enlightens everyone. There is nowhere it does not shine. It can pierce the stoniest recesses of the heart. It must, however, be consciously chosen. It does not force its way into any caves in which we may choose to retreat. All who choose to accept it share in the light and spread it. Some, however, prefer darkness to light. Later in the gospel, Jesus says to Nicodemus, "the light has come into the world, and people loved darkness rather than light because their deeds were evil. For all who do evil hate the light and do not come to the light, so that their deeds may not be exposed" (3:19-20, NRSV). This dualistic contrast does not account, however, for the fact that no one walks totally in the light or completely in the darkness. There is always something more in us that needs to be brought to the light.

Second, while the light shines in us, we ourselves are not the light itself. Like John, we are illumined by the true light and we testify to it, inviting others into its brilliance, but we know we are not the source of the light. It is through God's desire and divine initiative that we share in this life and light as children of God (vv. 12-13).

Third, no matter how deep the darkness, it cannot overcome the light (1:5). There is no individual or collective sinfulness that is able to extinguish the divine light. The opening phrase of the gospel recalls the opening line of the book of Genesis, which introduces the first creation account. Most likely written in postexilic times, it asserts that although the nation has considered itself guilty and punished in Babylon for its unfaithfulness, God considers humankind, along with all creation, to be very good (Gen 1:31). The gospel assures us we are always capable of letting ourselves be brought to the light. Like the rescued miners, we are offered the way out of darkness and now must be willing to testify to the power of the light within us.

PRAYING WITH SCRIPTURE

1. Invite the Light of the World to shine more brightly in you.

2. How do you testify to that light?

3. Ask Christ to illumine anything that keeps you in darkness.

FLEEING FOR LIFE

The Holy Family of Jesus, Mary, and Joseph

Readings: Sir 3:2-6, 12-14; Ps 128:1-2, 3, 4-5; Col 3:12-21; Matt 2:13-15, 19-23

"Rise, take the child and his mother, flee to Egypt" (Matt 2:13)

Four years ago, Fermina López, a native of Guatemala, found herself divorced, homeless, and jobless, with three children to raise. She felt she had no choice but to flee her beloved homeland and make the perilous journey north in search of work. She was one of the lucky ones who survived the five-day trek across the desert and found employment in Phoenix. When she was able to save enough money for smuggler fees, she sent for her children one by one, whom she had left in the care of her neighbors. The first two made it, but her youngest, who got as far as the US-Mexican border in July 2010, is now feared dead. The López family is one small unit among the 214 million international migrants in the world today, a number that has doubled in the last three decades. Not all have achieved their dreams for a life no longer threatened by death from political opponents or military regimes or inadequate economic resources.

Today's gospel tells of Joseph's dream, in which a divine messenger relays Herod's intent to kill the infant Jesus. The angel instructs Joseph to flee with Mary and the child to Egypt, a traditional place of refuge for Israelites (e.g., Gen 42–48; 1 Kgs 11:40; Jer 26:21). They too faced a treacherous desert crossing, though the gospel tells none of those details. We can only imagine Mary and Joseph's fear as they stole away under the cover of darkness and all the hardships they endured. Matthew says nothing about what happened when they arrived in a strange place, having to navigate in an unfamiliar language and culture. Who helped them along the way? How did Joseph find work? What did Mary think about Joseph's dreams? The evangelist skips ahead to the Holy Family's departure from Egypt, quoting

Hosea 11:1, "Out of Egypt I called my son." As he is wont to do, Matthew interprets all that happens in the life of Jesus as fulfillment of Scripture. By identifying Jesus with Moses and the exodus, he introduces the theme that Jesus is the new authoritative teacher of the law.

Just as Moses received a divine command to return home after the death of those who sought his life (Exod 4:19), so Joseph follows the angel's command to return home after the death of Herod the Great. Herod's sons, however, still pose a threat. Archelaus, the eldest, inherited Judea, Samaria, and Idumea, which he ruled for ten years (4 BCE–6 CE). Philip governed the area north and east of the Sea of Galilee, and Herod Antipas controlled Galilee and Perea. Archelaus was no less cruel than his father, so Joseph is fearful of returning to Judea. Once again he is directed by an angel in a dream, and he settles his family in the more peaceful Galilee. It may have been the availability of work in Sepphoris, the city being built by Herod Antipas as his capital, that led Joseph to settle his family in Nazareth, some four miles away. As usual, Matthew interprets this move as fulfillment of Scripture. Matthew's meaning is puzzling, however, since there is no text in the Scriptures that says, "He shall be called a Nazorean." It is likely that he intends an allusion to Isaiah 11:1, which speaks of a shoot (*netzer*) that will sprout from the stump of Jesse, thus highlighting Jesus' royal Davidic lineage.

The experience of the Holy Family of having to flee for their lives into a foreign land gives strength and courage to millions of today's migrants. Those living in the host country are challenged by the gospel to consider what kind of welcome they would want to offer to newcomers if they were none other than Jesus' own family.

PRAYING WITH SCRIPTURE

1. Pray for justice and compassion toward immigrants.

2. Listen for God's directives for how to preserve the life of the most vulnerable.

3. For what do you dream? Talk with God about it.

A MOTHER'S WORK

**The Blessed Virgin Mary,
Mother of God**

Readings: Num 6:22-27; Ps 67:2-3, 5, 6, 8;
Gal 4:4-7; Luke 2:16-21

*"The Lord look upon you kindly and
give you peace!"* (Num 6:26)

The founder of Mothers Against War wears a button that reads, "War Undoes Mothers' Work." Our liturgical celebration today likewise juxtaposes Mary, the Mother of God, and prayer for world peace. Today's readings speak to us of God's motherly love and offer Jesus' mother as an example for how that maternal care becomes enfleshed in humankind. The feast today is not a sentimental exaltation of motherhood, but offers guidance for how men and women alike can engage in maternal work that averts war and builds peace in the human family.

The gospel is the same as that of Christmas Day, but on this feast day, while we are still celebrating the birth of Christ, our attention is drawn to Mary. She receives the divine message from visiting shepherds, proclaiming glory to God and peace for all peoples on earth. Mary keeps in her heart all that she has heard, reflecting on it again and again. As at the annunciation (Luke 1:26-38), she does not fully understand what God is doing or asking of her, but the Spirit gives her the ability to say yes, trusting in the One who has always been faithful. She maintains this stance throughout her life, as also when she treasures everything in her heart after the disturbing episode of having found her twelve-year-old son among the teachers in the temple (Luke 2:51). A fundamental attitude for bringing to birth God's dream of peace for us is to live like Mary, in contemplative wonder, dwelling in mystery, trusting in the ways of the Holy One.

Another key ingredient in building peace is highlighted in the first reading and in the psalm response. They invite us to live in a stance of blessedness, accepting that we are blessed and beloved of God, which then enables us to extend blessing to all peoples. Mary exemplifies this stance, when at the visitation, she receives blessing through Elizabeth, who exclaims that Mary and the child she carries are blessed. Elizabeth also blesses Mary for believing that there would be fulfillment of what was spoken to her by the divine messenger (Luke 1:39-45). As the gospel continues, Mary's son, taught well by his mother, helps his disciples know how to live in blessedness. "Love your enemies, do good to those who hate you, bless those who curse you, pray for those who abuse you," he says (Luke 6:27-28, NRSV). Disciples who live this way reflect divine parental love. As "children of the Most High," they emulate the One who is "kind to the ungrateful and the wicked" (Luke 6:35, NRSV).

In the second reading, Paul, speaking to a community of Gentile Christians, uses the metaphor of adopted children to assure them of their equal stance as begotten of God and heirs to all the divine promises. In the context of today's feast, we might read this as an invitation to regard all people as children of God, our brothers and sisters, all embraced by God's boundless love. The Spirit not only helps us cry out to God as our own parent but also helps us to hear this same cry on the lips of our siblings throughout the globe. The Spirit helps us to seek only good for all our siblings and to find ways other than war to resolve our differences.

In 1968, when Pope Paul VI first asked that January 1 be observed each year as a World Day of Peace, he noted that "the world must be educated to love Peace, to build it up and defend it." Peace building does not come as instinctively as maternal love, but both can be learned and taught. We can turn to Mary to show us the way to contemplate God's motherly love, to live in blessedness, and to teach others the ways of building peace.

PRAYING WITH SCRIPTURE

1. Spend some time in contemplation with the Giver of Peace.

2. Practice extending blessing to the person you find most difficult to love.

3. Choose to become more educated about peace building and share that with someone else.

ADOPTED IN LOVE

Second Sunday after Christmas

Readings: Sir 24:1-2, 8-12; Ps 147:12-13, 14-15, 19-20;
Eph 1:3-6, 15-18; John 1:1-18

"[A]mong my chosen put down your roots" (Sir 24:8)

Sister María del Carmen is a passionate Spaniard who came to San Cristóbal de las Casas, in the state of Chiapas, México, decades ago. She has worked tirelessly for the women of the diocese, teaching them the tools of biblical interpretation, social analysis, and networking, in order to help empower them for transformative change. Under her leadership, land was acquired, a center was built, and countless meetings have been held, bringing together women who were formerly voiceless and powerless. When asked how long she would stay in this mission land, she quickly retorts, "Here I have been called and here I will plant my bones when I die." Like her, missionaries the world over have left their homes to respond to God's call to serve a people not their own, falling so deeply in love with them that they cannot ever imagine leaving. They have adopted a people and the people have adopted them.

The readings today speak of Jesus' becoming human in similar terms. The letter to the Ephesians says that God adopts us through Christ. God has fallen in love with humankind, and, in Christ, pitches the divine tent in our midst, and here chooses to remain. The metaphor of adoption underscores that this love relationship is chosen; it did not have to be. This makes the adopted one even more beloved.

In the first reading, Woman Wisdom first speaks of being in the assembly of the Most High. There she seems perfectly happy, as she is exalted and admired in the midst of her people. But when the Creator directs her to pitch her tent in Israel, among God's chosen, there she readily goes and fixes her abode. God's chosen become her beloved as she declares, "I have struck root among a glorious people" and elects to linger in their company.

The Fourth Evangelist uses very similar language and imagery to speak of the Word becoming flesh. Like Woman Wisdom, the Word pitches his tent among the chosen ones to whom God sends him. While the author of the letter to the Ephesians used the metaphor of adoption to describe how we become God's beloved, the prologue of John's Gospel speaks of how we are born as children of God—"not of blood or of the will of the flesh or of the will of man" (1:13, NRSV), but by faith in the Word. "Not of blood" refers to the belief in antiquity that conception occurred through the mingling of woman's blood with male seed. Nor does being begotten by God come about through human desire, "will of the flesh," or, more precisely, that of males, "the will of man." In Jesus' day it was thought that males were the initiators of sexual activity.

The Fourth Evangelist asserts that although the Word that became flesh was a unique Son (1:14), all can become equally beloved children of God, by allowing themselves to be born anew through faith in the Word. Later in this same gospel, Jesus will invite Nicodemus into this rebirth (3:5). This rebirthing is a continual action on the part of God. It is not something that occurs only once. In this Christmas season, there is the delight and joy at the birth of the One who comes to abide with humankind. But in a few short months, we will journey with him again through another birth as he undergoes his passion and is then resurrected. Already today's gospel hints at this. Some of those with whom he chooses to dwell will not accept him (1:11) and will seek to end his life. When that time approaches, Jesus tells his disciples that the suffering they are about to endure are the birth pangs that will lead to another birth (16:20-21). Like a faithful missionary, he never leaves those with whom he has cast his lot; he remains with them in the form of the Paraclete (14:16-20; 20:22). Just as Woman Wisdom is not apart from the presence of the Creator when she dwells with Israel, so the Son is ever at the bosom of the Father (1:18) even when he has become human. So, too, those who believe in the Word are always reclining on the breast of Christ, as his Beloved Disciple (John 13:1), no matter where they are called to pitch their tent.

PRAYING WITH SCRIPTURE

1. When has love impelled you to leave your own home, physically or metaphorically, to devote yourself to someone else?

2. Think of someone who has adopted you and give thanks for the free gift of his or her love.

3. Rest in the bosom of God, giving thanks for the many rebirths in your life and for those yet to come.

ALL ARE WELCOME

The Epiphany of the Lord

Readings: Isa 60:1-6; Ps 72:1-2, 7-8, 10-11, 12-13;
Eph 3:2-3a, 5-6; Matt 2:1-12

"[T]hey all gather and come to you" (Isa 60:4)

Some years ago at a gathering of sisters who were discussing the decline in vocations, Jamie T. Phelps, OP, posed this question to the predominantly white group: What if I told you that there were two hundred healthy, energetic, faith-filled young women who were ready to join you tomorrow? Of course heads nodded and smiles revealed the warm welcome they would be accorded. Sister Jamie queried further: What if I told you the two hundred women were black? The sisters suddenly found themselves struggling with their response as they faced their own unconscious racism.

The sisters' experience may not have been far removed from that of the Matthean community, which was predominantly Jewish, struggling to welcome Gentile believers. This is the gospel in which Jesus emphatically warns his disciples, when he sends them out on mission, not to go anywhere near Gentiles or Samaritans but only to "the lost sheep of the house of Israel" (10:6, NRSV).

This is also the community that told the story of the Canaanite woman whom Jesus rebuffed when she pleaded with him to heal her daughter. He declared that he had been "sent only to the lost sheep of the house of Israel" (15:24, NRSV). Her faithful persistence helped him to see that his mission could embrace others beyond the borders of his own people. This openness to other people than Jews reaches a climax at the conclusion of the gospel, where the final words of the risen Christ are his instruction to go and make disciples of all nations (28:19).

This all-inclusive mission of Christ is already foreshadowed in the opening chapters of the gospel, where exotic visitors from the East are the first to do homage to Jesus. The term "magi" originally referred to a caste of

Persian priests. They were not kings themselves but served their king with skills such as interpreting dreams. In the gospel they also appear to be adept at interpreting the movement of the stars. Following the star, they are the first Gentiles to seek and recognize Jesus, offering their precious gifts to him. In so doing, they foreshadow the way Gentiles will flock to the Christian communities, bearing gifts for mission.

All the readings for today's feast underscore the welcome extended to all in God's embrace. Isaiah speaks of how peoples from every nation will stream toward the renewed Jerusalem, all bearing their gifts and proclaiming God's praises. The responsorial psalm likewise sings of how every nation on earth will adore God's Anointed One. The letter to the Ephesians emphasizes that "the Gentiles are coheirs, members of the same body, and copartners in the promise in Christ Jesus through the gospel" (3:6). There are no second-class members and no privileges for those who had priority in the faith. All are equal comembers.

The very insistence on the equal status of Gentiles, backed up with the assertion that this has now been revealed to the apostles and prophets by the Spirit, reveals the struggles of the early Christian communities to make this a reality. The difficulties in welcoming Gentiles have long ago been overcome, but others still face us today. What welcome is given to people of different races? to people of different socioeconomic strata? to women? to those whose marital status is irregular? to those of a different sexual orientation? Facing our prejudices and working to dismantle them is a most difficult task. It can take a lifetime, but it is possible to do with the help of the Spirit, who continues to reveal the copartnership of all in the body of Christ.

PRAYING WITH SCRIPTURE

1. Pray for the grace to welcome people unlike yourself into your faith community.

2. Ask for the Spirit's help to accept the gifts of "outsiders" who come with authentic faith.

3. Ask Jesus for the healing of any prejudices you recognize within yourself or your community.

GRASPED BY GOD'S HAND

The Baptism of the Lord

Readings: Isa 42:1-4, 6-7; Ps 29:1-2, 3-4, 3, 9-10;
Acts 10:34-38; Matt 3:13-17

> *"I have grasped you by the hand;*
> *I formed you, and set you*
> *as a covenant of the people"* (Isa 42:6)

A frequently used technique in action films is a scene where a person is in danger, slipping off a cliff, or a building, or some other perilous perch. Someone grasps the person by the hand and desperately tries to pull him or her to safety. This is one of the images Isaiah gives us: God grasps the chosen servant by the hand and hangs on for dear life.

Set in the context of the return of the exiles from Babylon, the divine promise is to pull Israel back out of confinement and darkness into light and justice through the agency of a chosen servant. Scholars have long debated the identity of this servant, who features in three more oracles in the book of Isaiah: 49:1-7; 50:4-10; 52:13–53:12. Some think the servant is to be understood as Israel collectively, others the prophet himself or another person who lived during the time of the prophet. Christians see Jesus as the fulfillment of this prophecy.

The purpose for which God calls the servant is for the "victory of justice." The servant is to bring forth justice to the nations and justice on the earth. A mission centered on "justice" often conjures up images of fiery denunciations of evil and demands for repentance. Instead, Isaiah speaks of the gentle manner of the "chosen one": "not crying out, not shouting, / not making his voice heard in the street. / A bruised reed he shall not break, / and a smoldering wick he shall not quench" (42:3-4). Where there is a spark of righteousness that is in danger of being extinguished, whether by weariness or oppression or sinfulness, the servant will tenderly fan it back into full flame.

Matthew describes Jesus' baptism in similar terms. Like the Servant in Isaiah, Jesus experiences the Spirit of God gently settling upon him. The image of a dove evokes peacefulness and possibilities for a new beginning. Just as in Genesis 8, where a dove brings Noah the signs of hope for new life, so Jesus' mission opens a new hope-filled chapter in the history of God's saving action. Jesus experiences a profound opening to God's love and pleasure in him, which enables him to lead others to know God's delight and love in them. This rapturous moment of joy is like having the heavens ripped open (Matt 3:16; Isa 63:19) as the divine love pierces through any barriers to the human heart. The powerful arm of the Holy One reaches out to grasp all of humanity by the hand, both to save from danger and to walk hand in hand like lovers forever.

Just as the mission of the servant is centered on justice, so Jesus is intent on fulfilling all righteousness (the word *dikaiosynē* in Greek can be translated as "justice" or "righteousness," and signifies right relation in every aspect). Matthew shows what God's righteousness looks like in the persons of Joseph (1:19), John the Baptist (21:32), and Jesus. Jesus teaches his disciples to thirst for righteousness (5:6), and to let their justice surpass that of other religious leaders (5:20), emulating that of God, whose grace is extended to both the just and the unjust (5:45). At times when Jesus encounters those who refuse the divine hand extended to them, his gentle ways turn confrontational and urgent (e.g., Matthew 23). But for those who are earnestly seeking the Holy One, as was Jesus when he came to John in the Jordan, God's firm and steady hand is readily grasped with saving power and an eternal pledge of love.

PRAYING WITH SCRIPTURE

1. How have you experienced God grasping you by the hand? Talk with God about that.

2. When have you helped another to know how beloved he or she is?

3. How are you and your faith community working to establish justice on the earth?

BEGONE, SATAN!

First Sunday of Lent

Readings: Gen 2:7-9; 3:1-7; Ps 51:3-4, 5-6, 12-13, 17;
Rom 5:12-19; Matt 4:1-11

"One does not live on bread alone,
but on every word that comes forth
from the mouth of God" (Matt 4:4)

It is the subtle way that temptation resembles truth that gets us. For people who have made a fundamental choice to accept God's invitation to orient their lives toward the divine love, those things that are blatantly evil do not hold allure. They are easily recognizable as wrong, and it does not take much effort to reject them. The real temptations are the ones that are just close enough to the truth that they appear good and beneficial.

The author of Genesis captures this sense in the etiological account of how sin entered the world. The serpent, the mythological embodiment of temptation, is described as the most cunning of all the animals. It is able to twist the truth just enough to plant seeds of doubt and open the way toward rationalization. At first the woman responds to the serpent by correcting the false version offered by the tempter, as she accurately conveys God's instructions. The tempter proceeds, oh so cleverly, to erode her fundamental orientation toward God and succeeds in getting her to shift her focus. Instead of seeking the Divine Giver, she now grasps at the enticing gifts.

The devil's tactics in the gospel are very similar. Jesus has just had a powerful experience at his baptism, of being filled with the Spirit and knowing in a profound way that he is God's beloved Son (Matt 3:17). It is this very sense of his identity that the tempter tries to undermine. First, the devil holds out this seductive image: surely the beloved Son is entitled to have all his hungers satisfied. Quoting Deuteronomy 8:3, Jesus instead focuses on his hunger for the word of God. Throughout the gospel, we see

21

him feeding God's hungry people with both physical and spiritual food (Matt 5:1–7:29; 14:13-21; 15:32-39; 26:26-30).

Next is the temptation to believe that if Jesus is truly the beloved Son, God would never let any harm come to him. God's angels would swoop down and rescue him before any danger could befall him. Again Jesus turns to the Scriptures, which enable him to recognize the falsity in the claim of the tempter. A third time the devil tries to derail Jesus' centeredness on God as the source of all power and the one deserving of worship. Yet again, Jesus clings to the word of God to overcome the wiles of the tempter.

Finally the devil departs when Jesus commands, "Get away, Satan!" But not for long. The temptations circle back again and again, as variations on the same theme. Midway through the gospel, we again hear Jesus say, "Get behind me, Satan!" (16:23, NRSV), when he is tempted by Peter to reject suffering as integral to his identity as beloved Son. Right to the end, as Jesus is dying on the cross, the devil's words are echoed by the passersby: "If you are the Son of God, come down from the cross" (27:40, NRSV). The chief priests, scribes, and the elders chant the same: "He trusts in God; let God deliver him now, if he wants to; for he said, 'I am God's Son'" (27:43, NRSV).

Finally, the bandits who were crucified with him taunt him the same way (27:44). Yet again on the cross, Jesus turns to the Scriptures and prayer to stay solidly grounded in his identity as God's beloved Son. The words of Psalm 22 sustain him through the challenges that try to undermine his expectations of how God would care for him. The final verse of today's gospel assures us that just as God's angels accompanied Jesus in his ordeals, so we are never abandoned in times of trial.

PRAYING WITH SCRIPTURE

1. How do prayer and the Scriptures help you stay centered in your identity as God's beloved?

2. What helps you to recognize the subtle falsehoods that come from the tempter?

3. How have you experienced God's presence in the midst of trials?

MOUNTAINTOP VISION

Second Sunday of Lent

Readings: Gen 12:1-4a; Ps 33:4-5, 18-19, 20, 22;
2 Tim 1:8b-10; Matt 17:1-9

*"And he was transfigured before them;
his face shone like the sun"* (Matt 17:2)

What really happened at the transfiguration? Each of the evangelists tells the story slightly differently, with his own theological emphases. Was it a miraculous glimpse of Jesus' heavenly glory? A temporary unveiling of his divine nature to give hope to his disciples? Or was it a recasting of a resurrection appearance story placed in the middle of the gospel? These and other theories have long been entertained by biblical scholars.

In Matthew's version, the radiance of Jesus' face and clothing and the brightness of the cloud that overshadows the disciples are highlighted. Coming on the heels of Jesus' teaching that he must suffer and die before being raised up (16:21), the brilliance underscores that Jesus, although executed as a criminal, is righteous. As Jesus had told his disciples, at the end of the age "the righteous will shine like the sun in the kingdom of their Father" (13:43, NRSV). The voice from the cloud likewise reaffirms Jesus' identity as God's beloved Son, upon whom divine favor rests (as at his baptism, 3:17). The admonition "listen to him" echoes Deuteronomy 18:15, and emphasizes that Jesus is the authentic interpreter of the Mosaic Law and the prophets. He is not replacing Moses and Elijah but continues the long line of faithful leaders.

The presence of Moses and Elijah recalls their powerful mountaintop experiences of God and hints that similar things happen there to Jesus. On Mount Sinai God spoke to Moses face-to-face, entrusting to him the commandments that would guide his people to live in faithfulness through the desert days ahead. The glory of God is reflected on Moses' own face as he returns to the difficult task of leadership (Exod 34:29). Elijah flees to the same mountain, when trying to escape the murderous intents of Jezebel. There God speaks to him in a "still, small voice," giving him the courage to go forward to anoint a new king and Elisha as his successor (1 Kgs 19). Likewise, Jesus is at a turning point in his mission. There are those who seek his life, as well as those who try to live faithfully God's law that he teaches. On the mountaintop, he is able to see with God's own vision the way forward in faithfulness.

Jesus' transforming experience also resonates with that of the Rev. Martin Luther King Jr., who on the night before he was assassinated declared that he had been to the mountaintop, and had seen the Promised Land. He set aside all fear and assured his followers that even if he were killed, as a people they will get to the Promised Land. God's transformative love radiates through a face determined to love no matter what the other's response. As Jesus had taught his disciples from a mountaintop about transforming enmity through love, so King reminded his followers to disarm police forces through loving nonviolent confrontation and to answer fire hoses with "a certain kind of fire that no water could put out."

King urged his listeners to continue to struggle for justice here and now, not only to wait for "long white robes over yonder." So, too, Jesus' radiant clothes in the gospel are not simply a glimpse of his own divine status but a vision of the way in which each beloved child of God is to be clothed here and now. King urged his followers to give themselves to this struggle until the end, saying, "Nothing would be more tragic than to stop at this point" (Memphis: April 3, 1968). For Jesus, nothing would have been more tragic than to stop with teaching, preaching, and healing in the Galilee. To bring transfigured life to completion for all, he continues on toward Jerusalem.

PRAYING WITH SCRIPTURE

1. Go to the mountaintop with Jesus. What vision do you see?

2. How does the mountaintop vision strengthen us for the desert journey to freedom?

3. Pray for God's transformative love to radiate through you by choosing to love no matter the other's response.

WATER FROM ANOTHER'S WELL

—————— **Third Sunday of Lent**

Readings: Exod 17:3-7; Ps 95:1-2, 6-7, 8-9;
Rom 5:1-2, 5-8; John 4:5-42

"[T]he water I shall give will become in [them]
a spring of water welling up to eternal life" (John 4:14)

It is said that the next major wars will be fought over water, not oil. There are growing concerns over the increasing demand for fresh, clean water as the supply is decreasing. Today's challenges about ensuring access to safe water for every human being is one entry point to reflection on today's gospel, which centers on thirst for living water that is eternally replenished.

The account opens with a tired and thirsty Jesus asking a woman of Samaria for water. Like millions of women who even today spend hours of their day collecting water, the Samaritan woman comes, perhaps for a second time that day, to draw water. Most women would come to the well early in the morning, not at the hottest part of the day.

Most likely the Fourth Evangelist intends the noontime detail to be taken symbolically. In this gospel, light signifies coming to belief, while darkness corresponds to unbelief. In contrast with the preceding story of Nicodemus, who came to Jesus at night, and who is unable to believe, the woman of Samaria comes at the brightest part of the day and will come to full belief.

Jesus and the woman enter into a deep theological conversation, laden with symbolism. As often happens in the Fourth Gospel, the two are cast as representative characters for the whole of their people. They begin by speaking of their thirsts, their shared human need, and this enables a conversation by which they can begin to break down the enmity between their two peoples. Elsewhere in the gospel, Jesus speaks of his thirst to draw all people to God through himself (12:32) and of his desire for all to be one (17:21).

Step by step Jesus and the woman reveal themselves more deeply to each other. They speak of some of their deepest thirsts: for worship, salvation, and the search for truth. They listen intently and allow their perceptions of the other to shift, just as we may need to change our former impressions of the Samaritan woman. The focus of the dialogue is not on her marital history nor is she said to be a sinner. Jesus does not tell her to go and sin no more, as he does to the man at the pool of Bethesda who had been paralyzed (John 5:14) or to the woman caught in adultery (John 8:11).

The woman's understanding of Jesus progresses from the simple observation that he is a Jew to pondering whether he is greater than Jacob. Another step is her recognition of him as a prophet when he uses the marital metaphor favored by Hosea to speak of the peoples' relationship with God. Finally, she arrives at the conclusion that Jesus is the Messiah, which she shares with her townspeople in question form, so that they too can enter into the process of discovery that will culminate in faith.

This encounter illustrates a process by which enmity can be transformed into friendship. The two start by focusing on common thirsts that spring from their shared humanity. They had to let go of their ingrained stereotypes of the other, and they had to stop avoiding each other. They had to be willing to stay in the conversation for a good deal of time and not give up when they stumbled over their differences. They had to be willing to overcome the objections of some of their own people. They had to be willing to stay with one another. As the waters of understanding wash away ignorance and fear, the gift of living water wells up within them, making each one a spring from which others who thirst may drink.

PRAYING WITH SCRIPTURE

1. Pray for the courage to discover the gift of living water in another's well.

2. Ask Jesus to deepen in you the desire to be one with all people, with whom you share a common thirst.

3. How do you conserve and share our precious water resources?

UNLIKELY LEADERS

Fourth Sunday of Lent

Readings: 1 Sam 16:1b, 6-7, 10-13a; Ps 23:1-3a, 3b-4, 5, 6; Eph 5:8-14; John 9:1-41

"It is unheard of that anyone ever opened the eyes of a person born blind" (John 9:32)

A world-transforming movement was born through the most unlikely leader. One morning in 1995, twelve-year-old Craig Kielburger was captivated by the story of Iqbal Masih, a South Asian boy sold into slavery at age four who lost his life for speaking out for children's rights. Craig gathered ten of his friends and the movement Free the Children was born. Today it engages over a million children in peer education in forty-five countries, and has been nominated for the Nobel Peace Prize.

In today's first reading, we hear of a similar unlikely choice of a leader. It goes against traditional thinking to look to the youngest to lead into the future. The prophet Samuel was sure that Eliab was the one to be anointed, but God instructed him not to judge by appearance, and invited him to see as God does, by looking into the heart.

Today's gospel is also about seeing with the heart and about the unlikely leadership of a man who had been born blind. By allowing the works of God to be made visible through him, he becomes able to lead others to faith, even if not all accept his testimony. This same thing can be said of Jesus—he is an unconventional leader in the eyes of other leaders, whose objections and denials end with their refusal to see the works of God being made visible through him.

The man who was blind is open to the simple instructions of Jesus. He allows Jesus to put mud on his eyes, an ancient technique thought to have curative properties, and he obediently goes to the pool of Siloam, washes, and comes back able to see. In the lengthy exchanges that follow, first with his neighbors and then with the Pharisees, the man becomes more and more able to see with his heart, understanding more and more clearly who Jesus is, and grows in his ability to lead others to faith. He moves from not knowing Jesus (v. 12) to recognizing him as a prophet (v. 17), a man of God (v. 31), the Son of Man (v. 38). In the end he worships him as Lord (v. 38).

The other characters in the narrative throw up one obstacle after another, tenaciously refusing to see. The neighbors first debate about the identity of the man, insisting they do not see what they see. When the healed man settles that issue, they shift to the question of how the healing was done. Resisting the explanation of the newly sighted man, they turn to their leaders, who pick up the debate with the question of how the cure was done. The Pharisees latch on to another obstacle: Jesus must be a sinner because he did the healing on a Sabbath. When they turn to the healed man for his interpretation, he counters with, "He is a prophet." Unpersuaded, the leaders then revert to questioning whether there had actually been any blindness. The parents confirm the identity of their son and his congenital blindness, but say no more, out of fear.

Coming back to the healed man, the leaders have now made up their minds about what they see: that Jesus is a sinner. They circle back to question the fact of the healing and how it was done. They shore up their certitude about what they know and what they see, claiming their faithfulness to Moses, and finally end by dismissing the healed man as a sinner too. What Jesus does is unheard of (v. 32). The person he calls to lead others to faith is unconventional. The logical arguments why it cannot be so are endless. Those who allow themselves to quell their objections and to see with the heart can lead the way into a transformed future.

PRAYING WITH SCRIPTURE

1. How are your Lenten practices helping you to see with the heart?

2. What are your objections to seeing as Jesus sees?

3. What has never been done before that you see as possible?

BEING THERE

Fifth Sunday of Lent

Readings: Ezek 37:12-14; Ps 130:1-2, 3-4, 5-6, 7-8;
Rom 8:8-11; John 11:1-45

*"Lord, if you had been here,
my brother would not have died"* (John 11:21, 32)

One thing you want to be able to depend upon is that your loved ones will be with you in time of need. Therefore, the most puzzling part of today's gospel is that Jesus does not go right away to be with his dear friend Lazarus and his sisters after he receives word of Lazarus's illness. Why does he delay? The text does not answer that question directly. Even after Martha says to him forthrightly, "Lord, if you had been here, my brother would not have died," Jesus does not explain why he stayed away for two more days before deciding to come to Bethany. Mary confronts Jesus with the very same complaint (v. 32). Later, the onlookers ask, "Could not the one who opened the eyes of the blind man have done something so that this man would not have died?" (v. 37). The troubling question, voiced three times, is, Where is Jesus when you need him?

It adds to the puzzlement that at other times in the Gospel of John Jesus does come to the aid of persons in need of healing: the royal official's son in Capernaum (4:46-54), a man who was paralyzed at the pool of Bethesda (5:1-18), and a man born blind (9:1-41) near the pool of Siloam. In each of these instances there appears to have been no prior relationship between Jesus and the one asking for healing. Jesus is simply "passing by" when he sees the man born blind (9:1). The man healed at Bethesda does not know who Jesus is (5:11, 13). In the case of the royal official, Jesus refers to him as part of "you people" whom he disparages because of their desire for signs and wonders (4:48). Why would Jesus extend himself to these people and not to his close friends? He had once even put himself in danger by doing so in Bethesda, and that episode concludes with Jesus' opponents trying to kill him (5:18).

The two days Jesus delayed in going to Bethany may have been time that he needed to discern whether it was "the hour" for him to take this fatal step. It is clear that to go to Judea would put Jesus at great risk. His disciples twice try to dissuade him from going there (11:7-8, 12). Thomas's wry remark, "Let us also go, that we may die with him" (11:16, NRSV), proves to be exactly true; the chapter ends with the Sanhedrin planning to put Jesus to death (11:53).

As Jesus' followers try to build communities of equal disciples, it is a challenge to embrace as friends those who are not kin and those to whom we are not naturally drawn. It is even more difficult to be willing to lay down one's life for any of those befriended, as Jesus does. In the Fourth Gospel, Jesus' mission is to bring life to the full for all (10:10) by offering friendship to all persons and drawing them to himself (12:32). Jesus loves Martha, Mary, and Lazarus (vv. 3, 5, 35). But he also loves all other persons—to the death. There are no favorites or best friends. The anonymous Beloved Disciple stands for each person who allows himself or herself to be loved by Jesus and to love him in return. All of us beloved of Jesus can put ourselves in the place of the one who rests on Jesus' bosom (13:23).

When one chooses to abide in Jesus, then he is always present, even if not in the same physical, earthly way the first beloved disciples wanted him to be. As Martha professes her belief in the Risen One, she affirms that he is always truly present and that all who die believing in him are likewise living and present still. Such belief does not take away grief for the dear departed, but turns our mourning into hope-filled joy.

PRAYING WITH SCRIPTURE

1. Let Jesus hold you in his presence when it feels like he is absent.

2. How has Jesus helped you form risky friendships?

3. Share with Jesus whatever grief you may have over the death of a loved one and let him weep with you.

FOR THE FORGIVENESS OF SINS

—————— **Palm Sunday of the Lord's Passion**

Readings: Isa 50:4-7; Ps 22:8-9, 17-18, 19-20, 23-24;
Phil 2:6-11; Matt 26:14–27:66

> *"[T]his is my blood of the covenant,*
> *which will be shed on behalf of many*
> *for the forgiveness of sins"* (Matt 26:28)

Ask any Christian why Jesus died, and most will respond, "to save us from our sins." There are, in fact, a great many differing theological explanations for the death of Jesus in the New Testament. The Gospel of Matthew is the only one in which Jesus, with his words over the cup at the Last Supper, interprets his death in terms of forgiveness of sins (26:28). But in Matthew, Jesus' death is not framed as a sacrifice of atonement but rather the result of living a life of forgiving love and teaching others his way of forgiveness (5:38-48; 9:2-8; 6:12, 14-15; 18:23-35). Unique to Matthew is the fuller account of the treachery of Jesus' friend and disciple Judas, and his tragic end. A question is set before us, whether we, like Judas, will be incapable of accepting forgiveness or, like Peter, will be open to the forgiveness Jesus freely offers when we fail. Further, can believing communities embrace those who have sinned grievously?

There is a particular emphasis in Matthew's Gospel on the shedding of blood and its consequences, which reaches a climax in the passion narrative. Previously, Jesus had exposed the refusal of the religious leaders to recognize their complicity in the shedding of the blood of the prophets (23:30), just as Pilate tries to do when he washes his hands, declaring, "I am innocent of this man's blood" (27:24).

In contrast, the crowd responds with recognition that the effects of Jesus' execution will continue to redound not only upon them but also upon their children (27:25). This verse is most often read as an acceptance of responsibility or guilt for the death of Jesus. However, there is no verb in the sentence, making it possible to read it as a statement: His death is upon us and upon our children. It is a recognition that the effects of violence committed by leaders reverberate onto the people as a whole and continue to affect future generations. At the same time, with Jesus' words over the cup, Matthew asserts that the forgiving effects of the shedding of Jesus' blood also redound to them.

Jesus' invitation to drink from the cup of his "blood of the covenant, which is poured out for many for the forgiveness of sins" (26:28, NRSV), brings together two powerful symbols: blood and cup. Blood signifies the life force over which only God has power (Deut 12:23). The cup connotes suffering, as in Jesus' plea in Gethsemane, "let this cup pass from me" (26:39). By accepting Jesus' invitation to drink from the cup, disciples accept suffering that befalls them as a consequence of living the gospel.

At the same time, partaking of the blood signifies acceptance of the life force of God, which empowers disciples to endure and overcome suffering and evil. In the Gospel of Matthew this power is explicitly linked with forgiveness. Jesus has lived and taught forgiveness as a means of breaking cycles of violence. He has accepted "the cup" of opposition that such a life has engendered, which will culminate in his death. His own blood seals again God's covenant with God's people, just as Moses did with blood sprinkled on the people (Exod 24:8). The pouring out of Jesus' blood "for many" leaves no one out, as the Greek word *pollōn* reflects a Semitic expression where *many* is the opposite of *one*, thus the equivalent of "all." When the angel announces to Joseph, "he will save his people from their sins" (Matt 1:21, NRSV), it is not by a single sacrificial act but by an entire way of life into which his followers are invited.

PRAYING WITH SCRIPTURE

1. As we drink from the cup at Eucharist, pray for the ability to resist suffering that comes from abuse and injustice.

2. Drink in the life-giving power of God to withstand the suffering that comes from living the gospel.

3. Drink in the forgiving friendship of Jesus and extend it to another.

QUAKING WITH JOY

Easter Sunday

Readings: Acts 10:34a, 37-43; Ps 118:1-2,
16-17, 22-23; Col 3:1-4; Matt 28:1-10

"And behold, there was a great earthquake" (Matt 28:2)

As the people of Japan, Christchurch, and Haiti slowly rebuild their lives after suffering the devastating effects of earthquakes, a detail unique to Matthew's account of the empty tomb catches one's attention. The placid daybreak is shattered with "a great earthquake" (28:2), echoing the description of the aftermath of the death of Jesus found only in Matthew. Just after Jesus utters his final words and breathes his last, Matthew says, "The earth shook, and the rocks were split. The tombs also were opened, and many bodies of the saints who had fallen asleep were raised. After his resurrection they came out of the tombs and entered the holy city and appeared to many" (27:51-53, NRSV).

While the earthquakes of our day cause massive loss of life by entombing people in the rubble of collapsed buildings, the earthquakes in the gospel have the opposite effect: they split open tombs and raise to new life those held in the grip of death. They signal tectonic shifts made possible for humankind through God's action in Christ.

Foremost is the shift away from paralyzing fear to an empowering joy. The angel's first words to the women are "Do not be afraid!" (28:5). The centurion and those keeping watch over the crucified Jesus were terrified at the earthquake and what took place after his death (27:54), as were the guards at the tomb who "were shaken with fear" so that they "became like dead men." Not so Jesus' disciples. The angel directs them away from seeking Jesus the crucified so that they can experience him as risen. God's messenger invites them to come and see the place where he lay, but then directs them to go out quickly. They are not to stay in the place of death. They are not to build a monument to the martyr Jesus and glorify his death but rather to announce and live the new life that bursts forth from the empty grave.

Harboring some fear, they follow the angel's instructions, and let joy overtake them. Then Jesus himself appears to them and reiterates his oft-repeated invitation to his disciples to let go of the death grip of fear (Matt 8:26; 10:26, 28, 31; 14:27; 17:7). They can move from fear to joy, when they come to know that Jesus never abandons his earthquaked people and that he is able to transform even the most brutal effects of violence. It is not only in this one definitive act of raising the crucified Christ that God's life-giving power is exercised, but in every act of forgiveness and in every move toward reconciliation enacted by Jesus' disciples.

Easter is not only about what happened to Jesus but, to a great degree, it is about what happens to us as we live lives that are transformed by his rising. In his letter to the Colossians, Paul speaks about Christians being so united with Christ that when he dies, we die with him. And when he is raised, so we too. We not only await final transformation but, every time we stand with the crucified peoples of our day, as did Mary Magdalene and the other Mary, the Risen One is alive in us as we break the hold of death-dealing powers even now.

Poet laureate Maya Angelou captures this sense in her poem "Still I Rise," as she speaks about the past horrors of an enslaved people: "Up from a past that's rooted in pain / I rise / . . . Leaving behind the nights of terror and fear / I rise / Into a daybreak that's wondrously clear / I rise / . . . I am the dream and the hope of the slave. / I rise / I rise / I rise" (*And Still I Rise* [New York: Random House, 1978]).

PRAYING WITH SCRIPTURE

1. Out of what fear and pain is Jesus helping you to rise?

2. How do you and your faith community stand in solidarity with today's crucified peoples?

3. What is sealed in the tomb of your heart that God's angel wants to release?

CONSPIRATORIAL FAITH

Second Sunday of Easter

Readings: Acts 2:42-47; Ps 118:2-4, 13-15, 22-24;
1 Pet 1:3-9; John 20:19-31

"[H]e breathed on them and said to them,
'Receive the Holy Spirit' " (John 20:22)

An ancient way of determining when a person had died was to hold a glass mirror under the person's nostrils to detect any trace of moist air indicating that there was still some breath of life. Before modern methods of cardiopulmonary resuscitation (CPR), a person who had stopped breathing was simply allowed to slip away. In today's gospel, the risen Christ reinfuses the breath of life into the constricted lungs of the believing community, releasing them from the fear that choked their ability to breathe together and to live fully for his mission.

The frightened disciples are gathered behind locked doors "for fear of the Jews." In the aftermath of Jesus' execution, their fear is understandable—will they be next? In the Fourth Gospel, "the Jews" is code language for anyone who does not believe in and who opposes Jesus, even though Jesus himself and all his first disciples are Jews. The object of their fear is those who are like them in heritage, yet not like them in terms of belief in Jesus.

Sometimes what we fear most is seeing that which we do not want to face in ourselves reflected in "the other." Into the midst of this fearful space Jesus enters, inviting his disciples to accept the peace he desires for them. It is not a peace that ignores the brutality inflicted on him, as he shows them the still visible wounds. It is a peace that recognizes full well the horror of what has occurred and results from the willingness to enter into processes of healing, forgiveness, and reconciliation, rather than retaliatory violence. An ability to see the wounds differently, not as something that needed to be avenged but as something that Christ was already able to heal with his peace and his spirit, enables the disciples to let their fear give way to joy.

What results is a rebirth of the community. Just as the Creator brings to life the first human being by breathing into its nostrils (Gen 2:7), so the risen Christ brings back to life the frightened community of his followers. This is not a painless process. Recently, a friend suffered a collapsed lung. The intense pain he experienced when the lung was reinflated may be akin to the difficult process of transformation that Jesus' disciples had to undergo. Before his death, Jesus spoke to them about this pain as birth pangs that would give way to joy when the new life emerged (John 16:20-22).

For some this rebirth takes place on the first day of the week after the resurrection. But not all are present and not all are moving to the same rhythm. The next week there are still some who are locked in their fear and who set up what may appear as impossible conditions before they will come to believe. Thomas voices their doubts: They need to see with their own eyes and touch with their own hands. It is not so much a stubborn resistance to believe what others have experienced that Thomas expresses, as it is the necessity for each one to come to faith through a direct, personal encounter with Christ.

There can be no secondhand faith. The testimony of other believers leads one to Jesus, but it does not substitute for the tangible experience of Christ needed by each one. The gospel also allows that there are different ways that people come to faith: some through seeing, some without. Both are blessed. No matter how one comes to believe, it is with a "conspiratorial" faith community—people who "breathe together" through the Spirit, who dissolves fear by the use of peace, forgiveness, and reconciliation.

PRAYING WITH SCRIPTURE

1. As you pray, focus on your breath, welcoming the divine breath of life that dissolves fear.

2. What do you need to see and touch to come to greater belief?

3. How do you "conspire," "breathe together," with others in your believing community?

WALKING INTO HOPE

Third Sunday of Easter

Readings: Acts 2:14, 22-33; Ps 16:1-2, 5, 7-8, 9-10, 11; 1 Pet 1:17-21; Luke 24:13-35

"But we were hoping that he would be the one to redeem Israel" (Luke 24:21)

They are walking away from Jerusalem, away from the place where their hopes were shattered. Cleopas and his unnamed companion—perhaps his wife?—stride in the direction of Emmaus, known in Roman times as Nicopolis, "Victory City." They were in sore need of "victory."

As they tell the stranger who joins up with them, they were hoping that Jesus would be the victorious one, the one who could redeem them, but once again the Romans had crushed their hopes of liberation. As they go, they debate how to understand the things that have happened, blind to the Victorious One alongside them.

Today's gospel is a story of how Jesus' followers moved from expectant wishing to being grounded in true hope. What they had been wishing for was someone who would rescue them from bondage, someone who would singlehandedly transform their situation for them. Most likely they thought this would happen through a violent wresting of power.

What they got instead was a new story, a new way of seeing, and hearts inflamed with hope. The door was opened to a new way of being for them and for us that far transcended anything for which they had wished.

In 1990, three years before he became the first president of the Czech Republic, Vaclav Havel offered these reflections on hope: "Hope is a state of mind, not a state of the world. Either we have hope or we don't; it is a dimension of the soul . . . an orientation of the spirit . . . it is not the same thing as joy that things are going well . . . but rather an ability to work for something because it is good, not just because it stands a chance to succeed . . . Hope is not the conviction that something will turn out well, but the certainty that something makes sense, regardless of how it turns out" (Paul

Wilson, trans., *Disturbing the Peace: A Conversation with Karel Hvizdala* [New York: Knopf, 1990], 181). Havel captures poetically what Luke tells narratively about how hope began to burn in the hearts of Jesus' first followers. While blindly fleeing Jerusalem because things did not turn out well, according to their wishes, the disciples come to see that Jesus' death is not the end of all their wishful longings nor an isolated act that rescues them but is the culminating point of a whole way of life that embodies hope.

In the breaking of the bread, the disciples do not just see a changed Jesus, but they come to see the whole world as changed. Jesus has liberated them from sin and death, but the saving work is not completed until the disciples embrace his way of living eucharistically. Only when Jesus' followers live in such a way that they risk their own bodies being broken and blood poured out in love for others is hope fanned into flame. Cleopas and his companion are able to choose to return to Jerusalem, the city that kills the prophets (Luke 13:34) and could kill them, when their eyes become opened.

Sight is transformed not so much in one magical moment but in a lengthy process of praying and studying the Scriptures, of walking with others and struggling to understand from their perspective, of daily taking, blessing, breaking, and sharing bread in eucharistic gatherings, all the while urging Jesus to "stay with us." When a transformative moment happens, when we let go of our puny wishes and become aflame with hope, the Jesus we thought we knew vanishes, and the risen Christ remains.

In Jerusalem, Cleopas and his companion rejoin the gathered community who are likewise transformed. Together with the women who had gone to the tomb, and Simon, they see with new eyes and tell a new story, able now to lead others in the ongoing journey into hope.

PRAYING WITH SCRIPTURE

1. How is Easter hope different from fulfillment of wishes?

2. In what ways have Scripture study and Eucharist fanned the flames of hope in your faith community?

3. Ask Jesus to walk with you into Easter hope.

THE OPEN DOOR

Fourth Sunday of Easter

Readings: Acts 2:14a, 36-41; Ps 23:1-3a, 3b-4, 5, 6;
1 Pet 2:20b-25; John 10:1-10

"I am the gate for the sheep" (John 10:7)

Some years ago there was a television quiz show called *Let's Make a Deal*, in which contestants were given an opportunity to exchange a modest prize for a chance at a grand prize. Suspense built as they were asked to choose: door number one, door number two, or door number three. Two doors concealed a "zonk," or gag prize. Behind the third door was something very desirable like a trip, a car, or large amounts of cash. Every once in a while someone would get lucky and choose correctly.

In today's Gospel, Jesus speaks of himself as the door that leads to the most desirable of gifts. Unlike the quiz show designers, who for their own gain might deliberately try to mask the location of the grand prize, Jesus shows himself openly to be the gateway, and declares his desire for all to choose this door.

At the beginning of today's gospel selection, Jesus speaks about himself as the shepherd of the sheep who enters the sheepfold properly, through the gate. He contrasts himself to the thief or the robber who scrambles into the sheepfold some other way, and who will have no success in getting the sheep to follow him out. He is a stranger and the sheep will run away from him; they do not recognize his voice. Later in this chapter of John's gospel, Jesus elaborates further the image of himself as the Good Shepherd, but in today's gospel the focus is on himself as the gate for the sheep.

An important aspect of this image is that the gate swings in two directions. Not only do Jesus' followers come into the sheepfold through him but they are also led out by him. All who are led in by him find in the embrace of the believing community a place of refreshment and rest, a space where wounds can be healed, and where all can be nourished by the word and at the table. But whoever enters is also led out to find pasture, the verdant space of mission. Jesus is the gate that opens in and out.

Later in the gospel, the image of the open gate takes another form. Jesus' open side, pierced by the soldier's lance (19:34), also beckons us to enter, so that we can then go out in the power of his risen life. All who enter into his way of life, which offers the most forgotten and downtrodden verdant pastures of plenty, risk reprisals from those who try to enter another way. Even should one's life be taken for entering into this sheepfold, Jesus' open side also provides a portal outward to life birthed anew. Before his death, Jesus spoke to his disciples of his passion as labor pains that would give way to joy when the new life was born (16:20-22). The blood and water that flow from his open side recall the "rivers of living water" that Jesus promised would flow from within (literally, "from the womb of") him and from the heart of each believer (7:38, NRSV).

The open tomb on Easter morning completes the image. The gates of death have been breached by the One who came so that all "might have life and have it more abundantly" (10:10). The door now lies wide open for all. The invitation to enter through Jesus and his way of life is difficult for some to accept. The Pharisees, representing those who choose not to understand, do not accept Jesus' invitation to come in and go out with him and through him. They think there is another way over or around the gate. But there is no trick to choosing the correct door. It stands wide open before us.

PRAYING WITH SCRIPTURE

1. What is the "open door" that Jesus is inviting you to go through at the present time?

2. What form does coming in and going out of the gate that is Jesus take in your life?

3. Have you tried to climb in another way?

UNTROUBLED HEARTS

Fifth Sunday of Easter

Readings: Acts 6:1-7; Ps 33:1-2, 4-5, 18-19;
1 Pet 2:4-9; John 14:1-12

"Do not let your hearts be troubled. Believe in God,
believe also in me" (John 14:1, NRSV)

There are people who have the extraordinary gift of being able to exude a calm, unworried presence, even in the most trying of times. They are not oblivious to suffering and troubles, but they do not allow these to turn them into grim bearers of the glad tidings. Nor are they bright-eyed optimists who resolutely see the sunny side of every situation. It is not that they absolve themselves from involvement in caring for those who are suffering or from rectifying injustices. Rather, their outward joy is a reflection of a deep-seated hope and trust in God no matter what the circumstances. They have been able to take to heart in a profound way Jesus' admonition to his disciples in today's gospel: "Do not let your hearts be troubled." You know people like this. Are you one of them?

In today's gospel, Jesus not only exhorts his disciples to have untroubled hearts, but he helps them know how to find the way there. The setting is the Last Supper and the disciples have plenty good reasons to be distressed. Jesus has been speaking of going away and of being handed over and of being denied by two of his closest friends. The disciples are confused and anxious. Where is he going and how can they know the way to be with him? Unlike the Gospel of Mark, where a central question is, Who is this? (2:7; 4:41; 8:29), throughout the Fourth Gospel the prime concern is "where." The first potential disciples want to know, "where are you staying?" (1:38, NRSV). Jesus knows from where he has come and to where he is going, but his enemies do not (7:27; 8:14; 9:29). In Jesus' trial Pilate demands to know, "Where are you from?" (19:9, NRSV). At the empty tomb, Mary Magdalene's distress centers on Jesus' whereabouts: "we do not know where they have laid him" (20:2, NRSV; see also 20:13).

Throughout the Fourth Gospel, *where* does not refer to a geographical space but refers to inner communion with Jesus that rests on belief in God and belief in him. Jesus desires for his followers the same kind of indwelling that he enjoys with the Father, as he prays, "As you, Father, are in me and I am in you, may they also be in us" (17:21, NRSV). Oftentimes Jesus' assertions that there are many dwelling places in his Father's house and that he is going to prepare a place for the disciples (14:2) are taken literally. Some Christians envision a heavenly mansion, where Jesus is reserving "a room with a view" for those who are faithful to him. But, the dwelling place of which Jesus speaks is a profound union with him that is both a present reality and a continually deepening movement that will be brought to completion in the fullness of time.

This is not an easy thing to grasp, nor is it a facile journey. Yet in another sense, there is nothing more simple: Jesus himself is the Way. Thomas, who in John's Gospel always voices the believer's doubts and misunderstandings, blurts out, "Master, we do not know where you are going; how can we know the way?" (14:5). An easy sidestep is to claim not to know the way. Another diversionary tactic is voiced by Philip: "Master, show us the Father, and that will be enough for us" (14:8). His willingness to settle for a mere glimpse of the One who invites us into deep, abiding union is like stopping at a cheap motel when palatial accommodations are offered. We do know the way into the untroubled heart of God, and we have seen the fullness of the Divine visible in Jesus. Believing and following him, even in the face of death, our hearts can be "calmed and quieted . . . like a weaned child with its mother" (Ps 131:2, NRSV).

PRAYING WITH SCRIPTURE

1. Let Jesus, the Way, lead you into the place of deep indwelling with God.

2. What troubles your heart? Talk to Jesus about it.

3. Ask Jesus to lead you beyond your hesitations into that place that is prepared for you.

NEVER ALONE

Sixth Sunday of Easter

Readings: Acts 8:5-8, 14-17; Ps 66:1-3, 4-5,
6-7, 16, 20; 1 Pet 3:15-18; John 14:15-21

"I will not leave you orphans" (John 14:18)

The number of children worldwide who have lost parents is estimated at 133 million. The aid group SOS Children's Villages reports that every day 5,760 more children become orphans. In sub-Saharan Africa, some 15 million children have lost their parents to the AIDS epidemic. Millions become orphans because of national and international conflict and natural disasters. To meet their needs for security, a home, education, health care, and love is a daunting task. Frequently sprinkled throughout the Hebrew Scriptures are reminders to take care of orphans, who are usually linked with widows and foreigners, the most vulnerable in the society (e.g., Exod 22:21-22; Deut 24:19-22).

In this Sunday's gospel, which is part of the farewell discourse, Jesus assures his disciples he will not leave them orphaned. His impending departure will not leave them bereft of his love. They will not be homeless and will not need to be cared for by strangers. He promises to send "another Advocate" to be with them always. The Greek word *paraklētos*, "Paraclete," has a rich array of nuances. It literally means "called to the side" of another. It can have a legal sense, like "advocate," or "defense attorney." More generally, it can refer to a helper, mediator, or intercessor, one who appeals on another's behalf. Another nuance is that of "comforter," as expressed in the sequence for Pentecost, when we pray, "You, of comforters the best," and ask for rest, refreshment, and solace.

What is paradoxical in this last aspect is that the kind of consolation provided by the Comforter is not of the sort that wraps us in a warm, fuzzy cocoon and allows us to remain there forever. It is more akin to the loving nudge with which a mother bird impels her fledglings to take wing. As theologian Timothy Radcliffe, OP, puts it, "This is what the Holy Spirit does, thrusting us out of our ecclesiastical nest into mission" (*Why Go to Church? The Drama of the Eucharist* [London: Continuum, 2008], 198). In order to be able to be thrust out, the Consoler also gives us the sure realization that we are never abandoned. We have a home in the One who draws us ever more deeply into mutual indwelling: "you are in me and I in you" (14:20).

The first reading gives us a glimpse into what results when disciples make their home in Christ and allow the generativity of the Spirit to be unleashed. Stephen, chosen as a minister from among the Greek-speakers, esteemed as one "full of faith and the Holy Spirit" (Acts 6:5, NRSV), becomes fearless enough to go into the region of Samaria and there proclaim Christ. His intrepid venture among a people previously thought to be enemies impels Peter and John also to leave the nest in Jerusalem, and to continue Jesus' mission to the lost and forgotten. The Fourth Evangelist depicts the mission to Samaria begun by Jesus himself in an exchange with a woman at a well, who brings her townsfolk to believe in Jesus as savior of the world (John 4:4-42).

Jesus does not leave any orphaned. He is the embodiment of a motherly God who never forgets her children (Isa 49:15) and a fatherly God who protects orphans and widows (Ps 68:5). Just as parental love at its best is unconditional, so too is God's love. Although some translations of John 14:15 and 14:21 seem to imply that God's love and the sending of another Advocate are conditioned by human response, the focus is actually on the mutuality of the love. The divine love has been made manifest in God's gift of the Son (John 3:16); human love of God is expressed in the keeping of the commandments.

As Raymond Brown points out, "Love and keeping the commandments are actually two different facets of the same way of life. Love motivates the keeping of the commandments, and indeed love is the substance of Jesus' commandments" (John 13:34; *The Gospel According to John XIII–XXI*, AB29A [Garden City, NY: Doubleday, 1970], 646).

PRAYING WITH SCRIPTURE

1. How do you make your home in Jesus?

2. How does the Spirit nudge you out of the nest?

3. Ask the Paraclete to lead you to the orphaned ones who need your love.

STEPPING OUT ON THE WORD

———— **The Ascension of the Lord**

Readings: Acts 1:1-11; Ps 47:2-3, 6-7, 8-9;
Eph 1:17-23; Matt 28:16-20

"[Y]ou will receive power when the Holy Spirit comes upon you" (Acts 1:8)

In her book *Wouldn't Take Nothing for My Journey Now* (New York: Random House, 1993), poet laureate Maya Angelou tells of her memory of her grandmother, who raised her in the little town of Stamps, Arkansas. She describes her as "a tall cinnamon-colored woman with a deep, soft voice," whose difficult life caused her to rely utterly on the power of God. Angelou envisioned Mamma "standing thousands of feet up in the air on nothing visible," when she would draw herself up to her full six feet, clasp her hands behind her back, look up into a distant sky, and declare, "I will step out on the word of God." Angelou continues, "She would look up as if she could will herself into the heavens, and tell her family in particular and the world in general, 'I will step out on the word of God.'" "Immediately," Angelou recalls, "I could see her flung into space, moons at her feet and stars at her head, comets swirling around her. Naturally it wasn't difficult for me to have faith. I grew up knowing that the word of God has power" (pp. 73–74).

In today's readings, we have similar images of Jesus taken up into the sky, having spent an earthly lifetime stepping out on the word of God, indeed, enfleshing that divine word. The disciples want to know if now is the time when he is going to restore the kingdom to Israel (Acts 1:6). They have hopes and expectations for the future fixed in past experiences of God's saving hand in their history. Jesus does not directly answer their question, but points them to the power of the Holy Spirit, who will guide them to witness to his gospel courageously in new situations beyond what they can possibly imagine. As Jesus himself learned in his earthly sojourn, the *what* of the mission cannot fully be known, but only the *Who* that is always with and within those who are willing to trust and to witness to the divine love.

In the gospel, the turbulence experienced by the followers of Jesus in the time of transition after his death is reflected in the narrative. "The eleven" calls to mind the painful reality that "the Twelve" (10:5) are no more, as one betrayed Jesus and then ended his own life (Matt 27:5). Yet the thread of hope is sustained, as the story continues where Jesus' appearance to the women at the empty tomb left off. Mary Magdalene and the other Mary had seen and worshiped Jesus, and had been commissioned by him to tell the other disciples to go to Galilee, where they would see him (28:9-10). Today's gospel presumes that they have fulfilled this directive and the others have believed them, though nagging doubts persist (v. 17).

Another tension is evident in the reference to "eleven disciples." Disciples comprised a group larger than the Twelve (referred to seventy-three times in Matthew), among whom were, most notably, the Galilean women who followed and ministered (27:55). While Matthew has depicted the women as apostles who are commissioned in 28:7-10, he excludes them from the commission in today's gospel to preach to all the nations. Already tensions regarding women's witness surface.

Difficult, too, was the shift to a mission that would extend beyond Israel. Until this point in the gospel, Jesus had insisted that the disciples go only to the "lost sheep of the house of Israel" (10:5, NRSV; see also 15:24). Now the directive is to go to "all nations." The troubles stirred up by this new mission were myriad. The question of how law-observant Jewish Christians would be able to eat with Gentiles was only the tip of the iceberg. To weather such turbulent transitions, both in those early days of the church and now, the one surety is that Jesus is always with us (28:20 echoes 1:23), as we step out on the word of God in trust.

PRAYING WITH SCRIPTURE

1. Let Jesus lead you into the place where he is always with you.

2. How are you being asked to step out on the word of God?

3. How does the Spirit's power propel you into unknown territory?

GLORIOUS PRESENCE

Seventh Sunday of Easter

Readings: Acts 1:12-14; Ps 27:1, 4, 7-8;
1 Pet 4:13-16; John 17:1-11a

"I pray for them . . . I have been glorified in them" (John 17:9, 10)

"I'll pray for you" is a response that comes easily when we become aware of another person's particular need or difficulty. Some keep a list to help remind them of all those for whom they promise to pray. One time, a friend who has dedicated herself to a life of contemplative prayer knew that I was facing a particularly challenging situation and offered that she would hold me in prayer very concretely every day. She even extended the invitation that if there was a particular day and time that I would need special prayer, I could email her and let her know and she would be with me at that very time. This gift of prayerful presence and support sustained me in a powerful way and made God's spirit most tangible in a very trying time.

In like manner, Jesus prays for his disciples in today's gospel. The setting is the Last Supper, where Jesus has been speaking to his disciples about his impending departure, while also assuring them that the Paraclete will come to be with them. The prayer, while directed to the Father, is spoken in the hearing of the disciples, and concludes the Supper. It has three parts: Jesus prays first for himself (vv. 1-5), then for those who already believe in him (vv. 6-19), and finally for all future believers (vv. 20-26). We hear the first half of the prayer in today's reading.

The word that recurs again and again in the prayer and throughout the last part of the gospel is the noun "glory" (*doxa*) and its verb form, "glorify" (*doxazō*). It carries much the same meaning that the Hebrew word *kābôd* does in the Old Testament, where it refers to visible manifestations of God's majesty in acts of power. For example, when the needy Israelites are crossing the desert, they "see the glory of the LORD" in the manna God provides (Exod 16:7, NRSV). The notion that glory is a radiant, fiery substance comes from references such as Exodus 24:16-17, where Moses ascends Mount Sinai, and "the appearance of the glory of the LORD was like a devouring fire on the top of the mountain" (NRSV). Likewise, in Ezekiel's visions divine glory is described as gleaming brightness. But the root meaning of *kābôd* is "weightiness," that is, something impressive in a person that gives one importance, as in Genesis 13:2, where Abraham is said to be very "rich," literally, "heavy" or "glorious" (*kābēd*) in cattle, silver, and gold. Another example is Genesis 45:13, where Joseph asks his brothers to tell their father "how greatly . . . honored" (*kĕbôdî*) he is in Egypt.

In the Fourth Gospel, it is the Word become flesh and dwelling among us that makes the divine glory, God's impressive presence, visible to us (John 1:14). When Jesus begins to reveal his glory publicly in signs at the wedding feast of Cana, disciples perceive these as concrete manifestations of God's presence and come to believe in Jesus (2:11). Now, as he is about to depart, he speaks to God of how he has glorified God on earth, that is, has manifested the divine presence through his impressive deeds, and asks, "Now glorify me, Father, with you, with the glory that I had with you before the world began" (17:5). Here the language of glorification refers not so much to a fiery radiance that belongs to another realm but, rather, to the divine presence, manifest in diverse modes. Enjoying glory with God before the world began is a way of speaking of Jesus' being in the presence of and being one with the Creator from eternity (1:1-3). In his earthly sojourn, Jesus made visible in human form this divine presence ("I glorified you on earth" [17:4]). He is now entering another moment in his way of being with God and with humankind (17:11), and it is his disciples who will make visible God's presence on earth in the way that he did. Jesus is already abiding in them. He affirms this, saying, "I have been glorified in them" (17:10). This is similar to the way that the divine glory was said to be visible on the face of Moses after his encounter with God on Mount Sinai (Exod 34:29-35). Jesus' disciples, although abiding in his glorious presence, will face very difficult days ahead. In order for them to perceive his presence, his glory, in them, and to have the courage to manifest that publicly, he not only tells them he will pray for them, but does so in their presence. The prayer unleashes God's weighty, tangible presence in a new way, if one is open to receive this gift.

PRAYING WITH SCRIPTURE

1. How have you felt God's presence when another has prayed for you?

2. How have you experienced the presence of a loved one who has died when you are united in prayer?

3. Who most needs your prayer at this time?

UNLEASHING INNER POWER

Pentecost Sunday

Readings: Acts 2:1-11; Ps 104:1, 24, 29-30, 31, 34;
1 Cor 12:3b-7, 12-13; John 20:19-23

"Then there appeared to them tongues as of fire,
which parted and came to rest on each one of them" (Acts 2:3)

"The day will come when, after harnessing the winds, the tides, and gravitation, we shall harness for God the energies of Love. And on that day, for the second time in the history of the world, [humankind] will have discovered fire." So wrote Teilhard de Chardin in his book *Toward the Future* (Hyde Park, NY: New City Press, 1936, pp. 86–87). Properly speaking, human beings did not discover fire. We know from cosmologists that fire is at the very center of our universe, which burst forth some 15 billion years ago in a great burning explosion of light. What human beings did discover in the Early Stone Age was how to control fire for heating, cooking, and many other uses. Teilhard's likening our ability to harness the forces of love to that of controlling fire for good purposes taps into one of the metaphors used by Luke in today's first reading.

In the Acts of the Apostles, the metaphor of tongues of fire is used to describe the divine power unleashed in the disciples at Pentecost. Although some Christian artwork depicts this literally, with little flames hovering over the heads of the disciples, Luke is clearly using symbolic language that evokes the same earth-shattering experience of the Holy One by the Israelites at Sinai. Moses had brought the whole of the twelve tribes to the foot of the mountain to encounter God. The mountain was then "wrapped in smoke, because the LORD had descended upon it in fire" and "the whole mountain shook violently" (Exod 19:18, NRSV).

So, too, at Pentecost, the whole entourage of Jesus' followers were gathered together in one place, including the eleven, Jesus' mother and siblings, and the Galilean women (Acts 1:14). The believers numbered 120 persons

(Acts 1:15), a symbolic number for the full people. A strong driving wind fills the house, much as the mighty wind that swept over the chaotic waters at creation (Gen 1:2). The wind and fire are symbols evocative of re-creation, not only on a personal level, emboldening frightened followers, but also signals a rebirth on a cosmic scale that will result from their mission to ignite Christ's love everywhere.

Images of rebirth are strong in Paul's first letter to the Corinthians. Paul speaks about the groaning of the whole of creation, still in the throes of labor, as God's work of birthing new life continues unceasingly. He speaks also of how our groaning joins that of the cosmos, as we experience the pangs of redemption and hope coming to fruition through the Spirit's movement in and through us. Paul affirms that the Spirit herself echoes these inexpressible groanings, as she acts as a midwife, drawing forth the new life longing to emerge.

What is notable about the image of birthing that Paul uses to speak about the unleashing of the power of the Spirit is that it concurs with the direction in which the power of the cosmos moves. The movement of birth from inside the womb outward to life in the world mirrors the dynamic of the universe that is ever expanding, exploding with life from the center outward, in gorgeously creative, chaotic, irreplicable patterns. Pentecost, then, is not so much about the power of God coming from outside us down onto us but a releasing of the power that is already within us, breathed into us by God at creation (Gen 2:7) and by the risen Christ still among us (John 20:22). As the gospel affirms, it is particularly through acts of forgiveness that we can harness for God the energies of love, setting a contagious fire for the re-creation that is groaning to emerge.

PRAYING WITH SCRIPTURE

1. Allow the Spirit to groan within you for a rebirth of hope.

2. Reflect on how the Spirit enables us to hear one another across boundaries of difference, as in the Acts of the Apostles, in ways that deepen understanding.

3. Ask the Spirit to help you to pray when you do not know how.

A DANCE OF LOVE

The Solemnity of the Most Holy Trinity

Readings: Exod 34:4b-6, 8-9; Dan 3:52, 53, 54, 55;
2 Cor 13:11-13; John 3:16-18

"The grace of the Lord Jesus Christ
and the love of God
and the fellowship of the Holy Spirit be with all of you" (2 Cor 13:13)

There is a classic story told about St. Augustine, who was strolling along the seashore, struggling to comprehend the mystery of the Trinity. He encountered a youngster with a little pail. The boy trekked back and forth, emptying bucket after bucket into a hole in the sand, a short distance from the shoreline. When Augustine asked him what he was doing, the lad replied that he was putting the ocean into the hole. When Augustine told him that was impossible, the boy responded that it was just as impossible for him to comprehend the mystery of the Trinity.

Augustine himself affirms that if we think we have understood, then what we have understood is not God (*Sermon* 117.5). While Augustine's insights are indeed true, this does not mean that we cannot know anything about the triune God. We strain to express in words and images and symbols what we have experienced of God, knowing that we cannot ever capture in our paltry expressions everything about who God is.

Moreover, we cannot know God *in se*, that is, in God's own self, but only in relationship to us. When Moses was struggling to know how to name God to his fellow Israelites, God responded in terms of how the Holy One was ever present: "I will be with you as Who I Am" (see Exod 3:14). At the same time, the enigmatic Tetragrammaton, YHWH, can also be translated, "I am Who I Am," or "I am the One Who Causes to Be what comes into existence," capturing also something of God's being and God's doing.

In the exchange between Moses and YHWH in today's first reading, Moses entreats God to "come along in our company" and "receive us as your own." This plea voices the desire of our hearts to experience God with us and for us and to know ourselves as belonging in the divine embrace. For Christians, the experience of God-with-us comes to its fullest expression in the unfathomable divine love enfleshed in the person of Jesus and the ever abiding Spirit. Today's gospel tells of God's ecstatic love for the world that overflows in the gift of the Son. He was sent not to die but to share the life and love that is the very essence of the Holy One-in-Three.

While much of Christian art depicts the relationship among the three persons as triangular or in a linear procession, an ancient term from the Eastern church fathers, *perichōrēsis*, can help us envision the dynamic love relationship of the Trinity in circular fashion. This Greek word means, literally, "going around," and suggests a vigorous dance-like movement—each person circling, interweaving, whirling in vibrant interaction with the others. The point of this dance of love, however, is not for the sole enjoyment of the divine Dancers. The dance is an open circle that invites all onto the dance floor, drawing them right into the midst of the energetic flow of divine delight. If some hesitate, preferring to sit on the sidelines, the Three-in-One circle back again and again, extending the invitation over and over to each and to all, changing the pace and the rhythm, so that even the most clumsy of us can learn the steps in the dance of divine love.

Paul suggests some practice steps for the dance: rejoice, mend your ways, encourage one another, seek agreement, live in peace, greet one another with a holy kiss. In these ways, we help one another onto the dance floor, where we become one with the very Source of grace, love, and communion.

PRAYING WITH SCRIPTURE

1. Pray with the image of *perichōrēsis* and let yourself join the circle dance of expanding love.

2. Use one of the translations of YHWH as a mantra, and let the divine "I Am" be revealed in you.

3. Give thanks for God's self-emptying love, as expressed in John 3:16.

CONSUMED BY CHRIST'S LIFE

The Solemnity of the Most Holy Body and Blood of Christ

Readings: Deut 8:2-3, 14b-16a; Ps 147:12-13, 14-15, 19-20; 1 Cor 10:16-17; John 6:51-58

"[W]e, though many, are one body" (1 Cor 10:17)

Scientists tell us that we are literally connected to one another and to all that is part of one vast web of life in our universe. It is not a metaphor or a symbol; it is literally true that the material of all of our bodies is intrinsically related because they emerged from and are caught up in a single energetic event that is the unfolding of the universe. Our common ancestry stretches back through the life forms and into the stars, back to the primeval explosion of light that began our universe. Atoms that may have been part of Jesus' body are now part of our bodies.

Today's readings invite us to claim this interconnectedness with Christ and with one another, for the ongoing life and flourishing of the world. In the gospel Jesus urges his followers to eat his flesh and drink his blood. The phrase "flesh and blood" is a way of expressing the totality of a person; believers partake wholly in the full being of Christ. At the same time, this language of eating flesh and drinking blood is offensive. The Greek word *trōgein*, "eat," in verse 54 is a very graphic one that literally means "to gnaw," or "to munch." Moreover, in other places in the Scriptures, "eater of flesh" is an expression applied to an adversary who is seeking to destroy a person (Ps 27:2). Drinking blood would be equally abhorrent to Jesus' disciples, as blood is regarded as the life force over which only God has power, and is therefore not to be consumed by humans (Gen 9:4; Deut 12:23; Acts 15:20). Eating flesh and drinking blood is also a way of speaking of brutal slaughter (Jer 19:9; 46:10; Ezek 39:17). It is no wonder that some of Jesus' disciples found this saying too difficult and decided they would no longer follow him (John 6:60-66).

The Bread of Life discourse is immediately followed by the note that Jesus did not wish to go about in Judea because his opponents were looking for an opportunity to kill him (John 7:1). Likewise, the Synoptic Gospels connect Jesus' gift of his flesh and blood to his impending death (Matt 26:26-29 // Mark 14:22-25 // Luke 22:14-23).

This context gives us some insight into the meaning of Jesus' offer of his flesh and blood for us to eat and drink. When his own flesh and blood are about to be devoured in brutal slaughter, he preempts this act by offering his flesh and blood, the whole of his being, to those who believe in his manner of bringing life to the world. Who and what he is cannot be consumed or annihilated by those who would want to inhibit the life-giving forces Jesus has unleashed in the world. When his disciples take in and become all that he is, the life forces he enfleshed continue to be offered for the life of the world.

In recent years a number of experiments have shown the power of groups who intentionally focus their energy on undermining violent forces and effecting peace. One such project was the National Demonstration Project in Washington, DC. During the two months of the summer of 1993 that a group of four thousand persons meditated, the rate of violent crimes dropped by as much as 48 percent. It immediately rose again after they stopped meditating (see http://www.istpp.org/crime_prevention/; for other similar experiments see http://www.worldpeaceproject.org/news/index.php).

The interconnectedness of all persons and all life in the body of Christ is not simply an abstract concept; it is palpable and visible. One can choose to be a destructive eater of flesh and drinker of blood, or to consume and be consumed by the One whose intent is for the ongoing life of the whole world.

PRAYING WITH SCRIPTURE

1. As you say "Amen" when receiving Communion, let it be "yes" to our interconnectedness with Christ and with the whole of the cosmos.

2. Let yourself be consumed by the power for life that Christ unleashes in us.

3. Envision peace and direct Christ's life force to situations in need of transformative love.

GLIMPSES OF HEAVEN

——— **The Solemnity of All Saints**

Readings: Rev 7:2-4, 9-14; Ps 24:1-2, 3-4, 5-6;
1 John 3:1-3; Matt 5:1-12a

"[W]hat we shall be has not yet been revealed" (1 John 3:2)

In a recent article in *Newsweek Magazine,* Dr. Eben Alexander, a neuro-surgeon who had a near-death experience, describes his journey into the afterlife ("Heaven Is Real: A Doctor's Experience with the Afterlife," Oct. 8, 2012). He tells of shimmering beings who gave voice to a booming and glorious chant, so filled with joy were they that they had to let it out in song. He experienced a sublime oneness, where everything was distinct, yet also part of everything else. A beautiful being that exuded friendship spoke without words this message: "You are loved and cherished, dearly, forever. You have nothing to fear. There is nothing you can do wrong."

Since time immemorial human beings have speculated about what awaits us beyond death. Some have concluded that there is no real existence beyond our earthly one. Others are sure there must be ultimate reward for those who try to do good and eternal punishment for those who act in deter-minedly wicked ways. Not a few have had experiences like Dr. Alexander. What they report is startlingly consistent: an experience of light, joy, and overwhelming love that encompasses them.

There are strong resonances between the vision of the seer of Revelation in today's first reading, and the experiences described by those who have been in near-death states: there is whiteness and angelic beings singing joyfully. For Christians, the source of joy is the One who has completed the journey through death, has arisen to new life, and promises the same to us. Belief in this promise, however, makes us no less curious about what, pre-cisely, lies beyond this life. Today's readings give us glimpses of it, a reas-surance, and a pathway toward it.

In the first reading, the seer of Revelation has a vision of the divine protective power at work on earth, keeping safe the land, sea, trees, and all the servants of God. The latter are sealed on their foreheads—marking them as belonging to and protected by God. The amazing thing in the vision is that it includes everyone—not only the full number of Israelites (v. 4), but also "a great multitude, which no one could count, from every nation, race, people, and tongue" (v. 9). The "one hundred and forty-four thousand" (v. 4) is not a finite, limited number, but is symbolic of totality: twelve symbolizing completeness (e.g., all twelve tribes of Israel), multiplied by completeness, and multiplied again by a number too large to count (1,000).

The second part of the vision is a glimpse of the heavenly liturgy, with the immeasurable throng from all the corners of the earth adorned in white robes and holding palm branches, symbols of purity and victory. They are crying out in praise of God and the Lamb (Christ), the source of their salvation. Whatever they have done wrong in life is now purged. They have allowed themselves to be washed "in the blood of the Lamb" (v. 14).

In the second reading is an assurance that we need not wait until the afterlife to experience the immense love of God—it has already been bestowed on us. No more intimate relationship could be imagined by the author of 1 John than that of mother and daughter, father and son. So is God's love for us now. As for what is to come, "what we shall be has not yet been revealed," but as God's own progeny, we shall continue to carry the divine likeness. But our seeing will be different. Then we shall see God as God truly is. Everyone who has this hope strives for purity, as God is pure.

The gospel picks up on that thread, spelling out the way to strive for purity—purity of heart that is manifest in comforting those who mourn, acting with meekness, hungering and thirsting for righteousness, acting mercifully, building peace, and enduring persecution for Jesus' sake. When we strive to live in this way, we catch glimpses of heaven already on earth, which one day will be brought to fullness. How the imperfections in us will be purged and what precisely lies ahead are yet to be fully revealed, but we have nothing to fear, as we have been assured, not only by experiences such as that of Dr. Alexander, but by the constant message of Christ that we are totally loved, and that love can cleanse us of all that keeps God's love from being fully realized. We take hope, too, from all those who have lived saintly lives, those known and unknown, who now live in the full embrace of God.

PRAYING WITH SCRIPTURE

1. Envision yourself standing with the immeasurable throng, robed in white, singing God's praise, and let the Holy One envelop you in love.

2. Ask the risen Christ to remove any fear that keeps you from living in a beatitudinal way.

3. Acknowledge the wrongs you have done and receive forgiveness that frees you to love more fully.

THE LAMB OF GOD

Second Sunday in Ordinary Time

Readings: Isa 49:3, 5-6; Ps 40:2, 4, 7-8, 8-9, 10;
1 Cor 1:1-3; John 1:29-34

"Behold, the Lamb of God, who takes away the sin of the world" (John 1:29)

As we return to Ordinary Time, the readings bring us back into reflection on the beginnings of our journey of discipleship. The liturgical cycle is not a circle that keeps us going around and around, repeatedly going over the same ground. Rather, each year, we approach the texts with freshness because our world is not the same as in the previous year and we ourselves have changed. Much as a couple, when celebrating their anniversary, retell the story of how they first met and fell in love, so the gospel invites us to reflect on the beginnings of how we came to know Jesus.

John the Baptist, who plays the role of best man (3:29-30), sets the stage for the first disciples to recognize and follow Jesus. His proclamation of Jesus as Lamb of God has caused much debate among scholars. For some, this title evokes the servant in Isaiah, spoken of in today's first reading. In subsequent chapters, there is emphasis on the suffering of the servant, who is oppressed and afflicted, "yet he did not open his mouth; like a lamb that is led to the slaughter" (Isa 53:7, NRSV). Others think of the lambs sacrificed in the temple as sin offerings (Lev 4:32-35). Still others think of the Passover lamb, whose blood was smeared on the doorposts of the Israelites the night before beginning their exodus from Egypt (Exod 12:1-13).

One difficulty with the first interpretation is that it fits better the Synoptic Gospels than the Gospel of John. In the Synoptic tradition, Jesus does not answer back throughout his trial and stands before his accusers in silence. In the Fourth Gospel, however, Jesus is depicted as fully aware and even in control of the events in the passion narrative. He does not remain silent but answers back in a confrontational manner when he is struck (18:23). In the book of Revelation, the victorious Lamb completes the picture begun in the Gospel of John.

Neither is the symbol of a sacrificial lamb the best fit for the Gospel of John. Jesus stops the sacrificial process in the temple, driving out the sheep and the cattle (2:13-22). Moreover, in this gospel, he speaks of himself not as an unwitting victim, but as the gate for the sheep and as the shepherd who willingly lays down his life for his sheep (10:7-18).

Most likely it is the symbolism of the Passover lamb that the Evangelist intends. Just as in the exodus, the lamb's blood protects the people as they begin their arduous journey toward new life. At the death of Jesus, the Evangelist brings this symbolism to the fore again, by interpreting the decision not to break Jesus' legs, as they did to the other two crucified with him, as a fulfillment of the Scriptures that refer to the Passover lamb: "None of his bones shall be broken" (John 19:36, NRSV; cf. Exod 12:46). As the new Passover lamb, Jesus protects his disciples (17:11-15) and opens the way for the new liberation of his people.

It is not as an expiatory sacrificial lamb that Jesus takes away the sin of the world, but as one who embodies a way of life that frees people from all sinfulness that holds them bound. He shares with his disciples the power to live this manner of life when he appears to them after the resurrection, breathing the Spirit upon them and commissioning them: "If you forgive the sins of any, they are forgiven them" (20:23, NRSV). Just as John predicts in today's gospel, Jesus bathes his followers with the Holy Spirit, enabling us to live as he did, forgiving everyone we can. Living in this way extends John's testimony to the Lamb of God in our day, and continues Christ's action of taking away the sin of the whole world.

PRAYING WITH SCRIPTURE

1. Who first pointed you toward Jesus? Give thanks for that gift.

2. To whom do you testify about Jesus?

3. How do you experience the power of the Spirit to forgive?

THE LIGHT OF HOPE

Third Sunday in Ordinary Time

Readings: Isa 8:23–9:3; Ps 27:1, 4, 13-14;
1 Cor 1:10-13, 17; Matt 4:12-23

*"The people who walked in darkness
have seen a great light"* (Isa 9:2)

For those of us living in the Northern Hemisphere, this is a season of short days and increased darkness. For some, it triggers depression brought on by chemical changes in the brain due to light deprivation. To help guard against this malady, some leave their Christmas lights burning far into the winter. Others flee to the south, to bask in the sun and the warmth. Today's readings center on the light of God's saving action that has dispelled the darkness of destruction and death. In the first reading, the light refers to the reversal of fortunes for Israel after the Syro-Ephraimite crisis (ca. 733 BCE), when the Assyrian invaders overtook the area of the northern tribes. In the gospel, this same text is quoted, this time to refer to the light that has dawned with the coming of Jesus.

In the section immediately preceding today's gospel, Jesus had been forty days in the desert, fasting, resisting the temptations of the devil, quoting Scripture, and being ministered to by angels. These preparations make him ready to begin his prophetic ministry. The Gospel of John notes that after Jesus' baptism, he spent time baptizing in the Judean countryside, while John was baptizing at Aenon near Salim (John 3:22-23), a location likely in Samaria. Matthew's Gospel picks up the story with John having been arrested, which prompts Jesus to return to the Galilee. It is likely that John had moved on to the Galilee with his baptizing ministry, since it is Herod, tetrarch of Galilee, who imprisons him (Matt 14:1-12). The reason for Jesus' return to Galilee may have been to pick up where John left off. This is an ominous move. Jesus does not go to his hometown of Nazareth, a sleepy village of a few hundred families, but to Capernaum, a bustling fishing town on the shore of the Sea of Galilee. It was located at the cross-roads of the territories of Herod and Philip, along the Via Maris, the "Way of the Sea," the international trade route that connected Damascus and Syria with Phoenicia and Egypt. This was a strategic choice by Jesus. The light he would ignite with his preaching, teaching, and healing would have a far greater reach from such a locale.

One of the first things the gospels recount is that, like moths drawn to a light, others are attracted by Jesus' invitation to share in "catching" people in the net of the reign of God that is now at hand. It is a communal endeavor. In today's Gospel, two pairs of brothers are called. In Luke's Gospel, Mary from Magdala, another important fishing village on the shore of the Sea of Galilee, follows Jesus and ministers along with Joanna, Susanna, and many other Galilean women (Luke 8:2-3). Their healing has prompted them to join Jesus to be agents of healing for others. The response of the disciples in today's gospel also initiates radical changes in their lives. They leave their occupation, though they bring their skills with them to be used in a new way. There are also changes in their family relationships, as the relationship with Jesus and devotion to his mission becomes their primary focus. While it is said that James and John left their father, later episodes in the gospel imply that in the case of Peter, his family home becomes a hub for the mission, in which his family members play an important role (e.g., Matt 8:14-17). Together, Jesus and his disciples spread the light of hope for those who struggle against the despair of disease, illness, and sin. The forces that tried to extinguish this light in John will be no more successful in doing so with Jesus and his followers.

PRAYING WITH SCRIPTURE

1. How do the ways in which you proclaim the gospel fan hope into flame for others?

2. What are the forces that try to extinguish the light of hope?

3. How does the unity to which Paul exhorts us in the second reading spread light?

HAPPINESS NOW

Fourth Sunday in Ordinary Time

Readings: Zeph 2:3; 3:12-13; Ps 146:6-7, 8-9, 9-10;
1 Cor 1:26-31; Matt 5:1-12a

"Rejoice and be glad,
for your reward will be great" (Matt 5:12)

In Charles Dickens's famous tale *A Christmas Carol*, the miserly Ebenezer Scrooge is visited on Christmas Eve by the ghost of his partner Jacob Marley, and is then shown three ghostly scenes from the past, present, and future. This experience brings about Scrooge's transformation from an utterly stingy person who has no compassion for his fellow human beings into a man who awakes on Christmas morning full of hope that the dire scenes he has witnessed can yet be changed. His acts of benevolence to the family of his employee Bob Cratchit and his reconnection with his nephew's family fill him with joy and goodwill toward all.

How do we find fulfillment and joy when the effects of sin and strife have marred the past and when hunger, poverty, devastation of the planet, ongoing wars, and terrorism point to a bleak future? In today's gospel Jesus sums up in eight statements a way of life that brings true happiness and blessing already in the present, along with the promise of fullness of joy in days to come. There is nothing terribly new in this teaching. The prophets and wisdom teachers before Jesus spoke in a similar manner (e.g., Prov 3:13; 28:14; Sir 25:7-9; Isa 30:18; 32:20). Each statement of the Beatitudes begins, *makarioi hoi*, "Blessed (or "happy") are those who . . ." Each is in the third-person plural, indicating communal action and relationship. The first thing the Beatitudes tell us, then, is that living them is not an individual pursuit.

The Beatitudes name the ways in which peoples' happiness is threatened: grinding poverty (*ptōchos* in v. 3 denotes "beggar," one who is destitute), grief, landlessness, hunger, war, and persecution. Jesus does not advise that those so afflicted simply wait for a reversal of fortune in the hereafter, though the final verse does speak of great reward in heaven.

Jesus also counsels attitudes and actions that will bring about the reign of God, already tasted in the present. To be poor in spirit is not to accept poverty as an inevitable state of life, but rather to find one's wealth in God, to trust in God's care for the poor (Exod 22:25-27; Isa 61:1), and to seek righteousness, which rectifies the unequal distribution of goods, so that all have enough to thrive.

To be meek is not to be shrinking violets who accept injustice but, rather, to know our proper place as children of God and to insure that all are treated as full heirs to God's realm. To be peace builders, we are to engage in acts of mercy and forgiveness, which cleanse the heart and allow us to see God in the faces of our brothers and sisters here and now. And like the grieving women who went to the tomb of Jesus, we do not mourn in despair when we suffer loss, but we allow our sorrow to be transformed by hope in the Risen One.

Such a manner of life is able to heal the hurtful memories of the past and to transform the present toward a hope-filled future. This is not proposed as an intense form of Christianity meant for only a few select persons. Jesus addresses this teaching to all his disciples and to a great crowd, inviting them to recognize their capacity for happiness in the present by espousing attitudes and actions that will influence the future.

Jesus' teaching is different from the often-quoted maxim of Nathaniel Hawthorne (1804–64): "Happiness is a butterfly, which, when pursued, is always just beyond your grasp, but which, if you will sit down quietly, may alight upon you." Happiness is available to us when we pursue Jesus' manner of living, which is already within our grasp.

PRAYING WITH SCRIPTURE

1. As you pray, choose one of the Beatitudes for your focus. How will you live it today?

2. Ask Jesus to release you from any "ghosts" of the past that keep you from living in the happiness of the Beatitudes.

3. What blessing lies deepest in your heart?

UNDILUTED AND UNDIMMED

Fifth Sunday in Ordinary Time

Readings: Isa 58:7-10; Ps 112:4-5, 6-7, 8-9;
1 Cor 2:1-5; Matt 5:13-16

"You are the salt of the earth" (Matt 5:14)

Today if we say someone is "the salt of the earth," we understand that person to be solid and dependable, someone who can be counted on through thick and thin. We might also say that someone's speech is salty to mean that their language is coarse, like that of a sailor who has been out to sea for a long time and who has not had to be concerned about using polite expressions in refined company. But when Jesus said to his disciples that they were the salt of the earth, they might have understood the metaphor in light of several biblical connotations.

First, salt was a critical necessity for human life, along with water, fire, and iron, as Sirach 39:26 states. Salt was important for seasoning and preserving food. Job questions, "Can that which is tasteless be eaten without salt?" (Job 6:6, NRSV).

A second way in which salt was important was for liturgical functions. It was included with cereal offerings (Lev 2:13) and burnt offerings (Ezek 43:24). Blending salt with incense kept the fragrant powder pure and sacred (Exod 30:35). Salt was what Elisha used to purify a polluted spring of water (2 Kgs 2:19-22). In Catholic liturgical tradition, the baptismal ritual included putting salt on the infant's tongue, as a symbol of incorruptibility.

Another way in which salt was used was to ratify covenants (Num 18:19; 2 Chr 13:5). As a preservative, salt symbolized the lasting nature of the agreement.

Finally, different kinds of salts are necessary for the soil to be fruitful, but soil that has been "burned out by sulfur and salt" is a desert wasteland (Deut 29:22, NRSV; cf. Ps 107:34; Job 39:6). As a symbol of permanent destruction, conquerors would spread salt on a city they had razed (Judg 9:45).

As Jesus called his disciples "salt," they may have understood any of these meanings: they season and purify the world with God's love, giving witness to divine fidelity that preserves life for all eternity.

Jesus then queries, "But if salt loses its taste, with what can it be seasoned?" (Matt 5:13). It seems like a trick question. Salt can be diluted, but could it ever lose its taste entirely? It is possible that Jesus was quoting an ancient proverb to which his disciples would respond, "Impossible!" In the Talmud there is an account of Rabbi Joshua ben Hananya (ca. 80–120 CE) who was asked by philosophers in the Atheneum at Rome, "If salt becomes savorless, with what can it be salted?" He responded, "With an after-birth of a mule" (*b. Bek.* 8b). The point is that just as it is impossible for a mule to give birth, or for salt to become insipid, so disciples cannot cease to be who they are and to season the world with the good news.

The accompanying image of disciples as light reinforces the message. As impossible as it is for a city set on a mountain to be hidden, and as unthinkable as wasting fuel to light a lamp only to extinguish it immediately, so inconceivable is it that disciples would cease to let their light shine before others. Although trials and tribulations may threaten to dilute disciples' "saltiness" or dim their light, nothing is ever able to take away their capacity to illumine God's love for others.

Finally, salt and light are most effective when they do not call attention to themselves. Just as in well-seasoned food the salt is not noticeable and in a properly lit room the lamps are not the focus of attention, so disciples' good deeds do not redound to themselves but lead others to glorify God.

PRAYING WITH SCRIPTURE

1. Talk to Jesus about things that threaten to dilute your "saltiness" as his disciple.

2. How does Jesus help you keep your light burning brightly?

3. How do your good deeds point to the Source of light and not feed your own glory?

THE LEAST AND THE GREATEST

Sixth Sunday in Ordinary Time

Readings: Sir 15:15-20; Ps 119:1-2, 4-5, 17-18, 33-34;
1 Cor 2:6-10; Matt 5:17-37

*"[W]hoever obeys and teaches [the least of] these commandments
will be called greatest in the kingdom of heaven"* (Matt 5:19)

It begins with the tiniest gesture: an interested glance, the brush of a hand. Lifelong love builds from little expressions of care before it becomes total self-surrender to the beloved. At the opposite end of the spectrum, egregious acts of murder, betrayal, rejection, and deception begin with little sparks of anger, white lies, lustful looks. In today's gospel, Jesus instructs his disciples to watch out for the little things that undermine their love relationships.

The gospel belies any notion that Jesus overturns the Mosaic law or that the God of the Old Testament is a harsh God who issues strict commandments, while the God of the New Testament is a God of love and mercy. It is the one and the same God of bountiful mercy who gave the law, to whom Jesus is devoted. Jesus insists on the enduring value of the law, and his intent to fulfill the tiniest part of it.

What is new is his interpretation of the law, which at times was at odds with that of other religious leaders of his day. His is not a lax interpretation, but one that is even more demanding than theirs. To truly keep the law, one must go beyond it. Jesus speaks to his disciples about the little things that can erode their relationship with God and others and escalate into major offenses.

The formula "You have heard that it was said" introduces each of four commandments; this is followed by Jesus' invitation to go deeper: "But I say to you . . ." First, he speaks of taking steps to defuse anger before it reaches a murderous stage. He gives three concrete examples. Primary is to avoid insulting one another. Then, if there has been a rupture in a relationship, a ritual action alone will not mend it. A face-to-face reconciliation must be sought. Finally, conflicts should not be allowed to escalate to the point of litigation. In this section, Jesus is not speaking about justifiable anger at an unjust situation that gives energy to work for necessary change.

Just as anger can be the first step toward murder, so a lustful look can be the prelude to adultery, a form of which can be divorce. As with justifiable anger, Jesus recognizes situations in which divorce is a righteous action. It is not clear whether *porneia* (v. 32) connotes sexual misconduct, that is, adultery, or whether it refers to marriage to close kin, which was forbidden in Jewish law (Lev 18:6-18; see also Acts 15:20, 29).

The final section centers on honesty in relationships. If Leviticus 19:12 admonished, "You shall not swear falsely by my name, profaning the name of your God," Jesus says that relations among Christians should be so transparent that there is no need for taking oaths at all (NRSV).

By instructing his disciples to watch out for the little transgressions, he did not intend to frighten them into obeying a God who was lying in wait to punish them for every pecadillo. Rather, he alerts his followers that little slights, left unchecked, can lead to major offenses, with dire consequences. By the same token, great love and greatness in God's reign begin with little acts of love toward the least brother or sister. One saint who epitomizes this teaching is St. Therese of Lisieux. Through her "little way," she resolved to love all those she encountered in all the routine and ordinary interchanges of everyday life. Her greatness was recognized by her canonization only twenty-eight years after her death and the bestowal of the title of doctor of the church a century later.

PRAYING WITH SCRIPTURE

1. How can great love grow from little acts?

2. How can great conflicts be dissolved through small steps toward forgiving and reconciling?

3. In what little way will you express your great love of God today?

HAVING NO ENEMIES

Seventh Sunday in Ordinary Time

Readings: Lev 19:1-2, 17-18; Ps 103:1-2, 3-4, 8, 10, 12-13;
1 Cor 3:16-23; Matt 5:38-48

*"[L]ove your enemies
and pray for those who persecute you"* (Matt 5:44)

It is with great sadness that we received news on January 24, 2011, of the death of Don Samuel Ruiz, who had been bishop of the Diocese of San Cristóbal de las Casas in southern México from 1960 to 2000. Don Samuel is well known for having empowered the indigenous people of his diocese and for his role as mediator in the conflict between the Zapatista rebels and the Mexican government in the 1990s. For this, he had received many death threats. Some years ago I had the opportunity to meet him.

In the course of our conversation, I asked him how he had come to live so completely the command to love one's enemies, when he had so many. He gave me a puzzled look and responded, "I have no enemies." It was my turn to be puzzled, as he had arrived for the interview in a bulletproof van, accompanied by three large, armed bodyguards, supplied by the Mexican government, at their insistence! He explained further, "There are some who want to make themselves enemy to me, but I have no enemies."

In today's gospel, Jesus instructs his disciples on how to live in just such a way. Jesus begins by quoting the law of retaliation in Leviticus 24:20, which puts limits on acts of retribution, so as to curtail cycles of vengeance. The principle he puts forth is "do not retaliate (*antistēnai*) against the evil-doer" (see v. 39a). In some translations, the verb *antistēnai* is rendered "offer no resistance." But this verb most often carries the connotation of violent resistance or armed resistance in military encounters (e.g., Eph 6:13). Jesus is not advising his disciples to let evildoers freely abuse them; rather, he directs them not to retaliate by the same means. They are to respond with an action that confronts the evildoer nonviolently, thus breaking the cycle of violence and opening up a new possibility by which gestures of reconciliation can be reciprocated.

Jesus gives us four concrete examples (vv. 39b-42). The first involves a backhanded slap intended to humiliate (only the right hand would be used to strike another). Turning the other cheek is a provocative response that robs the aggressor of the power to shame, and instead the shame falls on the perpetrator. The second concerns a debtor, who stands naked in court, handing over not only the outer cloak demanded as collateral, but also the undergarments, a shocking act that places shame on the creditor (see Gen 9:20-27, where shame falls on Ham, the son of Noah who viewed his father's nakedness). The third instance likely involves a Roman soldier who has compelled a local person to carry his pack. The latter destabilizes the situation by creating a dilemma for the soldier, who would face punishment for exacting service for excessive distances. The fourth example is aimed at a person in a superior economic position. The context implies that the indebtedness is due to some injustice. The lender rectifies the situation by forgoing the demand for repayment. In each of these cases, nonviolent responses undermine enmity and open possibilities for new ways of relating. In this way the Mosaic law is fulfilled.

The last section deals with the command to love the neighbor (Lev 19:18). Nowhere in the Scriptures is there a command to hate the enemy. The question was whether one was obliged to act lovingly toward those outside the covenant community. Jesus' answer is affirmative. Disciples are to set no bounds on their love (*teleios* in v. 48 connotes not moral perfection, but "completeness, fullness"), just as God sets no bounds on the divine love.

PRAYING WITH SCRIPTURE

1. Pray for the grace to be able to say, "I have no enemies."

2. Ask Jesus to show you how to imitate God in setting no bounds on your love.

3. How do members of your faith community strengthen one another for transforming enmity into love?

DON'T WORRY, BE HAPPY!

Eighth Sunday in Ordinary Time

Readings: Isa 49:14-15; Ps 62:2-3, 6-7, 8-9;
1 Cor 4:1-5; Matt 6:24-34

*"[D]o not worry . . . seek first the kingdom of God
and his righteousness"* (Matt 6:25, 33)

Shortly after Bobby McFerrin's hit song "Don't Worry, Be Happy" won the Grammy Award for Song of the Year in 1989, I was invited to Jamaica to give a workshop on the gospel parables. Everywhere I went, the song was playing, and people were wearing T-shirts with the slogan, especially in the poorest barrios. I struggled to make sense of the irony: people living in grinding poverty with their smiling faces protesting happiness.

The saying "Don't worry, be happy" is attributed to Meher Baba, an Indian mystic and spiritual master (1894–1969), but it could just as well have derived from Jesus' words in today's gospel. Three times Jesus insists that disciples not worry, whether about life, food or drink, the body or clothing; and he urges reliance on Divine Providence.

How this instruction is heard and taken to heart depends on one's socio-economic position. To those who have all they need to eat, drink, wear, and sustain their bodily health, Jesus gives a warning not to center their efforts on accumulating more. Coupled with the introductory verses about serving God and not mammon, the gospel admonishes those who have enough of life's necessities not to give in to greedy desires that continue to escalate.

But what about those who are struggling just to survive, who truly worry about how they will feed their families? What good is it to voice assurances that God will provide? It would be especially pernicious if a person mired in poverty hears "O you of little faith" (v. 30) as an accusation that their neediness flows from their lack of trust in God.

The key can be found in verse 33, in which Jesus instructs his disciples, "seek first the kingdom of God and his righteousness, and all these things will be given you besides." When the focus of one's desires is on the right relations that characterize the reign of God, then those who have enough of life's necessities are not fixated on a quest for more. Rather, they cooperate with God in providing for those in need. Those who are poor can let go of their worries about survival, and those better off can be released from anxiety that derives from enslavement to possessions. These are the kinds of worries Jesus invites disciples to let go of. Worry on the part of those who are comfortable about others who are struggling can be a good and productive anxiety if it proves to be a catalyst to rectify unjust distribution of goods.

The gospel does not advocate that disciples should be passive in the face of genuine need, simply tossing off a happy-go-lucky assurance that God will provide. It is more akin to Meher Baba's fuller saying: "Do your best. Then, don't worry; be happy in My love. I will help you" (see "Baba's Words" by Frank Davis at http://www.avatarmeherbaba.org/erics/glossc-d.html).

The help that God provides is like that of a mother who could never forget her infant, as the first reading asserts. Likewise, the gospel speaks of God making motherly provisions by feeding and clothing not only her human children but also wild flowers and birds and grasses of the field. Since God is both fatherly provider (v. 32), who sows and reaps, and motherly caregiver, who feeds and clothes, all that has come forth from the divine womb is tenderly cared for before their needs are even voiced. As children of the Creator, we too tend and nurture all life, taking every measure possible to bring more fully to birth God's kingdom and divine righteousness, letting go of worry and entrusting ourselves to the One who wills true happiness for all.

PRAYING WITH SCRIPTURE

1. Talk to God about your worries. What response do you hear in prayer?

2. How does your care for the fragile creatures of Earth reflect God's tenderness for the children of her womb?

3. What is the meaning of "seek first the kingdom of God and his righteousness"?

SET ON ROCK

Ninth Sunday in Ordinary Time

Readings: Deut 11:18, 26-28; Ps 31:2-3, 3-4, 17, 25;
Rom 3:21-25, 28; Matt 7:21-27

"[The house] did not collapse; it had been set solidly on rock" (Matt 7:25)

It is certain that the rain, floods, and winds will come. Images of devastating floods in Haiti, Chiapas, New Orleans, Malaysia, Pakistan, Sri Lanka, and Queensland fill our news. When many of the places hardest hit are where the world's poorest people reside, the pleas to God in today's psalm to be a "rock of refuge" take on a literalness and an urgency. Sometimes preachers declare these disasters to be punishments from God and they urge people to repent of their sinfulness. These preachers espouse the kind of theology found in the Wisdom literature: that good things come to those who act uprightly, and that punishment awaits those who do not. The story of Job, of course, like that of Jesus, proves the inadequacy of this approach.

In the gospel today, Jesus presumes that rain, floods, and winds will occur, both literally and metaphorically. What he offers is not a theology about why these things happen, but a manner of life that enables believers to withstand all of life's challenges, and to be found upright when the final reckoning occurs (signaled by the phrase "on that day" in verse 22). The gospel is the concluding section of the Sermon on the Mount, on which we have been reflecting for the past several weeks. Jesus sums it up by saying that anyone "who listens to these words of mine," that is, the way that he interprets the Torah, and acts on them will be "set solidly on rock."

Two things are necessary to build this firm foundation: both hearing and doing the word. Listening is not enough. Nor is it adequate to simply proclaim Jesus as "Lord." Many times in the gospel, people in need cry out to Jesus as Lord to save them. "Jesus is Lord" was also an acclamation used in early Christian liturgies (Rom 10:9; 1 Cor 12:3; Phil 2:11). More is needed than calling on Jesus at times of crisis or acclaiming his power in liturgical gatherings. Doing the will of God by putting Jesus' words into action is also essential.

At the same time, Paul reminds us in today's second reading that being in right relation with God, self, and all creation does not depend on our own actions but on God's grace. This, Paul insists, is a free gift already accomplished by Christ. Our part is to believe. This faith is both having the conviction that God can and does accomplish in us the transformation wrought in and by Christ, and also acting in accord with the gift offered to us.

To hear the words of Jesus and put them into action requires an active choice, just as it did for the Israelites, as we hear in today's first reading, where Moses puts the choice to them concerning God's commandments. Today's readings invite us to examine our choices. Are we building on a rock-solid foundation by adopting daily practices that sharpen our hearing of the word and that impel us to act on it? Do we take a lesson from Peter, named "Rock": that, as for him, our surety can be a rock of stumbling, as when he rejected Jesus' hard words about his own suffering and death?

Three concrete actions for building our house on rock are given by Jesus earlier in the Sermon on the Mount: almsgiving, prayer, and fasting (Matt 6:1-6, 16-18). In prayer, we allow God to attune our ears to the divine voice echoed in all of creation, both in floods and calm. In fasting, we empty ourselves of our own desires, so as to hear the cries of those who hunger not by choice. In almsgiving, rather than shore up our own individual rocky perches, we become a rock of safety for those who are buffeted hardest by life's storms.

PRAYING WITH SCRIPTURE

1. How has God been a rock of safety for you in time of need?

2. In what spiritual practices do you engage in an effort to build your rock foundation?

3. How do your prayer, fasting, and almsgiving provide a rock of refuge for others in need?

LOVE CAN'T BE BOUGHT

Tenth Sunday in Ordinary Time

Readings: Hos 6:3-6; Ps 50:1, 8, 12-13, 14-15 (23b);
Rom 4:18-25; Matt 9:9-13

"[I]t is love that I desire, not sacrifice" (Hos 6:6)

"Money can't buy love" was the title of a recent advice column from a New York psychiatrist who was advising a middle-aged man who wanted tips on how to win a woman's love. He relayed that his present economic circumstances had changed and he was no longer able to afford expensive gifts to try to lure a mate. The psychiatrist observed that his approach of trying to buy love has more to do with power and control than with nurturing an authentic, intimate, loving relationship. She advised that he would need to change his whole approach, and be motivated by a desire to really get to know the other and let himself be known and loved in return. Then he could open himself to the possibility of true love, which cannot be acquired with money.

Today's readings similarly ask us to shift our approach toward the One who is wooing us into the most intimate of love relationships. In the first reading, God complains that the devotion of the whole people, from north (Ephraim) to south (Judah), is fleeting. Like the morning dew, it is superficial and evaporates quickly, not like the divine love that comes like the deeply saturating spring rain. What God desires from Israel is *hesed*, "mercy" or "loving kindness," and "knowledge" (*yādǎʿ*) of God, not sacrifice or holocausts. God pleads for love from the people that corresponds to that offered by the Holy One. *Hesed* is one of the words that most often describes God's love for Israel in the Old Testament. It is usually coupled with *ʾemeth*, "constancy," "faithfulness," "truthfulness." The word *yādǎʿ* connotes not only intellectual knowledge, but is often used for intimate relationships, and is even used as a euphemism for sexual intercourse. In contrast, sacrificial offerings can reflect an attitude of trying to buy divine favor: if I offer this sacrifice to God, then God will grant me what I desire (e.g., forgiveness, concrete signs of blessing, such as a good harvest, etc.). Hosea tries to direct the people to God's very self as the object of desire, and dislodges the notion that God's love can be earned or bought through their offerings.

In the gospel, Jesus echoes this same message, quoting Hosea's words, "I desire mercy, not sacrifice," when he is criticized for eating with tax collectors and sinners. He then says that he did not come to call the righteous but sinners. Jesus is not denigrating righteousness. In fact, in Matthew's Gospel, righteousness is a major theme and Jesus blesses those who hunger and thirst for it (5:6). He tells his disciples that their righteousness must exceed that of the scribes and Pharisees (5:20). He desires all to be "righteous," that is, in right relation with God, self, others, and the cosmos. His mission is to help those who are struggling most to find the path to righteousness. Like Hosea, he invites those who think they are righteous because they keep the law and offer the prescribed sacrifices to move to a deeper level of relationship, based on divine mercy. The measure of righteousness is the extent to which one emulates Jesus' love by accompanying those who are most in need of a divine physician.

Paul makes a similar argument to the Romans: righteousness cannot be earned through works but only through faith, as in the case of Abraham, who was said to be righteous (Gen 15:6), although he lived before the law was given. Righteousness, as Paul outlines it, is a free gift of God, accomplished by Christ. All we have to do is believe (Rom 3:23-26). Belief, however, is not simply intellectual assent, but works itself out through deeds of loving kindness (Gal 5:6).

In the advice column, the psychiatrist assured the man who wanted to know how to buy love that even though he was fifty-three years old, it was still possible for him to change. Hosea says the same to Israel, as does Jesus: it is never too late to let go of a sacrificial mentality and let the springs of divine mercy wash over us, overflowing in our expressions of faithful love toward God and neighbor.

PRAYING WITH SCRIPTURE

1. Talk to Jesus about the ways you find yourself trying to buy God's love. What does he say in response?

2. As you pray, let God's love, like the spring rain, saturate you through and through.

3. Do you think of yourself as mostly righteous or sinful? Ask Jesus what he desires for you.

DEARER THAN ALL OTHERS

Eleventh Sunday in Ordinary Time

Readings: Exod 19:2-6a; Ps 100:1-2, 3, 5 (3c);
Rom 5:6-11; Matt 9:36–10:8

"[Y]ou shall be my special possession,
dearer to me than all other people" (Exod 19:5)

At a funeral I recently attended, one of the daughters got up to give the eulogy. She began by saying, "I always knew that mom loved me best." I looked over at the faces of her two sisters and her brother, who seemed a bit disconcerted. The daughter went on to sketch out all the ways she knew she was her mom's favorite. Then she turned to her older sister and asserted, "I always knew she was mom's favorite," and then proceeded to tell all the reasons why. And so it went until she had recounted all the ways she knew her mom loved each of them the best.

In the first reading this Sunday, Israel wants to think of itself as God's special possession, dearer to God than all other people (v. 5). They believe this is true because of how God bore them up "on eagle wings" when they were fleeing the Egyptians. This reading was likely part of a covenant renewal ceremony, in which God's past saving deeds are recalled, as Israel recommits itself to the One who chose them and always remains faithful to them. Yet even as God speaks of the special relationship with the Israelites, there is a hint that God also loves others best at the same time, "though all the earth is mine."

Similarly, in the gospel, when Jesus summons the Twelve and sends them out to proclaim the nearness of God's reign and to heal and seek out the lost, these apostles may have thought that they were most specially chosen and loved. Indeed, they were. But they were also told to pray for the master of the harvest to send out more laborers. In other words, there are others who are just as loved and favored who are also called to share in the mission. When we think of the symbolism of the number twelve, we can see that twelve represents the whole people. Just as the whole of Israel consisted of twelve tribes, so the whole renewed people of God is symbolized in the Twelve chosen by Jesus. Just as all the Israelites were to be "a kingdom of priests, a holy nation" (Exod 19:6), so all of Jesus' disciples, symbolized by the Twelve, are called to make God present in the world, mediating the divine presence and holiness (a priestly function), and being agents of healing and reconciliation.

The daughter who gave the eulogy told of how some of the times she knew her mother loved her best were moments when she had been disobedient or had done something hurtful. It was the undeserved forgiveness and tenderness of her mom that convinced her she was the most beloved. This is the kind of loving mercy that Jesus' disciples have received and that he asks them to extend to others. It is not something that can be earned. "Without cost you have received; without cost you are to give" (Matt 10:8).

In Matthew's version of the sending of the Twelve, he instructs them not to go into pagan territory and not to enter a Samaritan town, but to go only "to the lost sheep of the house of Israel" (10:5-6). Later in Matthew's Gospel, Jesus reiterates to a Canaanite woman who wants her daughter healed that his mission is only to his own people (15:24). It is not until the end of the gospel that the Matthean Jesus sends his followers out to "make disciples of all nations" (28:19, NRSV). What began as a movement directed to one people who were specially chosen and loved by God soon expanded to become inclusive of all people, with the recognition that God's love is limitless and God loves each one best.

PRAYING WITH SCRIPTURE

1. Reflect on all the ways you know that God loves you best.

2. As you pray, join God in gazing with love at one whom you find difficult to regard as specially chosen.

3. How do you tend "lost sheep"?

FEARLESS FAITH

Twelfth Sunday in Ordinary Time

Readings: Jer 20:10-13; Ps 69:8-10, 14, 17, 33-35;
Rom 5:12-15; Matt 10:26-33

"[D]o not be afraid; you are worth more than many sparrows" (Matt 10:31)

"The only thing we have to fear is fear itself." This memorable opening line from the inaugural address of Franklin D. Roosevelt in 1933 lifted the hopes of a nation caught in the grips of the deepest economic depression it had ever experienced. Soon after, programs that aimed at relief, recovery, and reform were put into action and began to have the desired effects. In recent times, people who work in organizational change management have observed that fear, along with cynicism and judgment, is one of the greatest obstacles to creating new structures and relationships. Jesus seems to have recognized this long before FDR and modern-day facilitators. One of his most oft-repeated instructions in the gospels is "fear not."

These are similar to the opening words of today's gospel, repeated twice more in this short passage. It comes at the conclusion of the missionary discourse, as Jesus is sending out the Twelve to proclaim the good news, heal the sick, raise the dead, and cast out demons. He has instructed them to go with nothing: no bag, no clothes, no food, no money, but to rely on the hospitality of others, embodying power in vulnerability and communion in interdependence. He has warned them that they will be rejected by some, and even suffer physical abuse, and be handed over to the authorities. Jesus is not blind to the dangers of his mission and he does not want his disciples to be unprepared when they face these threats.

At the same time, he does not want them to be frightened off by these possible consequences. They are to proclaim the good news openly "from the housetops." And even if they should lose their physical life, this is not the most fearsome thing that can happen. Jesus then speaks to them of their supreme value in the eyes of God, as a reason not to be afraid. Just as God takes note of the tiniest creatures, such as sparrows, even more will divine care encompass Jesus' disciples. It is notable that Jesus does not tell them that God will intervene and rescue them from bodily harm. Should such befall them, however, they are not to give in to fear, because God will be with them and will preserve their life beyond bodily existence.

This gospel gives us an opportunity to reflect on what it is we most fear in following Jesus—not so as to fuel the fear by focusing on it but, rather, to acknowledge honestly what are our obstacles to proclaiming the gospel more fully with our lives. When we face our fears, voice them aloud to another, and surrender them to the One who has counted every hair on our heads, we can defuse their paralyzing power over us. Placing our full attention on the One who cares for us and empowers us, there comes a freedom beyond fear.

In the first reading, we see how Jeremiah was able to overcome the terror he experienced on every side, as even those who were his friends are looking for ways to trap him. He focuses on God's presence with him "like a mighty champion." As in the lament psalms, he pours out his complaint to God, knowing he is in the right and that those persecuting him are unjust. He relies on God to rectify the situation, and ends by praising God for accomplishing justice, as he knows God will do. In his fear, Jeremiah voices a desire that his opponents be put to lasting shame and that God take vengeance on them. His fear is transformed into praise and trust, as he places everything in God's hands, not acting out of fear or desire for vengeance, but from his confidence in God's saving power at work in him.

PRAYING WITH SCRIPTURE

1. Imagine the Holy One caring for sparrows and then let God tell you about your great worth in God's eyes.

2. Tell God about the fears you have and then surrender them into God's hands.

3. Conclude your prayer with praise and thanks, letting God's Spirit empower you.

FINDING LIFE

Thirteenth Sunday in Ordinary Time

Readings: 2 Kgs 4:8-11, 14-16a; Ps 89:2-3, 16-17, 18-19; Rom 6:3-4, 8-11; Matt 10:37-42

"[W]hoever loses his life for my sake will find it" (Matt 10:39)

For what or for whom would you be willing to give your life? Many people would answer that they would give their lives for their spouse or their children. Many a mother with a sick child has been heard to say that she would gladly take the illness upon herself rather than see her child suffer. In a community discussion about the choices women religious have made in responding to Vatican II, a sister in her golden years asserted, "I would give my life for who we are and what we have become and who we shall be in the future." She went on: "I have nothing to lose. When you get to be this age, you have become so in love with God and God's people, it's easy to pour out yourself in love."

In today's gospel, Jesus sets up a contrast: think of those most precious to you, such as your parents or your children. Just as your love for them has expanded your heart in such a way that you would do anything for them, even more does love for Jesus fill us to overflowing, so that those who follow him could pour out their very lives for Christ's little ones. To some people, such an other-centered life seems senseless, a loss of one's own autonomy and ability to pursue one's own desires. Paradoxically, the gospel message is that those who become schooled in losing their life in love for others actually find a life so fulfilling that any other way seems a waste.

Choosing this kind of life, however, is not entirely easy or without cost. Just as any love relationship flourishes only when both parties are willing to let their own desires, plans, and dreams be shaped by the other, leading to an ultimate surrender of self, so too does discipleship ask for such relinquishment. In the letting go, however, also comes finding of a new self that leads to joy and delight. Jesus is not asking for obliteration of self, as when people are trapped in systems of domination or poverty, where their sense of self is taken from them. He is speaking to disciples who are empowered persons who have the ability to choose to surrender themselves in love for his sake.

When Jesus speaks of rewards for receiving a prophet, or a righteous person, or for giving "a cup of cold water to one of these little ones . . . because the little one is a disciple," he is not talking about what his followers get for the sacrifices they make. These words come at the end of Jesus' address to the Twelve as he is sending them out on mission. He is referring to the reception they will get from others, and of the blessings that will come to those who open themselves to the apostles. Jesus describes a kind of domino effect. Anyone who receives his disciples receives Jesus and receives the one who sent him. Both those who are sent on mission and those who receive them are drawn into the circle of divine love.

Those who receive a prophet likewise participate in the prophetic ministry and its rewards. The prophet's reward is always twofold. Those who are being lifted up and empowered by the prophet's denunciations of injustice cheer the prophet's words and deeds. But those persons whose power, privilege, and status are threatened by the prophet's articulation of God's dream for righteousness will do all in their power to silence him or her. In some instances, as in the case of Jesus, and of the martyrs, this means that their physical life is taken. But, as Oscar Romero said the day before he died, "If they kill me, I will rise again in the Salvadoran people." Part of the reward of the prophet is arriving at a selflessness in knowing that God's word will be proclaimed by other prophets who will follow. Those who emulate prophet Jesus know that the prophet's reward is a transformation of self in the process of serving Christ's little ones, which culminates in the ultimate transformation into God's love for all eternity.

PRAYING WITH SCRIPTURE

1. How have you found life in giving of yourself?

2. How has costly love brought you joy?

3. Ask Christ to help you let go of anything that is not yet surrendered to him in love.

LIGHT BURDENS

—————— **Fourteenth Sunday in Ordinary Time**

Readings: Zech 9:9-10; Ps 145:1-2, 8-9, 10-11, 13-14;
Rom 8:9, 11-13; Matt 11:25-30

"[M]y yoke is easy, and my burden light" (Matt 11:30)

A mother balancing a child on one hip and a huge sack atop her head filled with items to sell in the market carefully makes her way through the crowded streets of La Paz. In addition to her physical load, she carries other burdens: economic stress, poor education, health challenges, racial discrimination. Like her sisters the world over, her daily life is characterized by valiant struggle against unimaginable obstacles.

When Jesus promises rest and an easy yoke in today's gospel, it is as if he knows precisely how such burdens feel. In this section of Matthew's Gospel, Jesus takes on the persona of Woman Wisdom, speaking with the words and images attributed to her in Proverbs, Wisdom, Sirach, and Baruch. In the verses preceding today's gospel, the witness of both Jesus and of John the Baptist is rejected, just as was that of Woman Wisdom (Sir 15:7-8; Wis 10:3; Bar 3:12). Jesus, identifying himself as Wisdom incarnate, concludes with the assertion, "Wisdom is vindicated by her deeds" (Matt 11:19, NRSV). This is followed by Jesus' denunciation of those towns that have rejected him (11:20-24). Today's gospel is the final section of this chapter, where Jesus, like Woman Wisdom, is a sage who reveals mysteries, interprets Torah, and calls disciples.

Jesus, like Wisdom (Sir 51:26), invites disciples to take up his yoke, that is, his instruction. In other places in Scripture, "yoke" signifies an oppressive burden unwillingly placed on the people's shoulders, like enslavement in Egypt (Lev 26:13) or exile in Babylon (Isa 47:6). God breaks such weighty bonds (Jer 2:20), and replaces them with the yoke of obedience to Torah. Similarly, to take up Jesus' yoke is to live by his interpretation of Torah. The lightness of Jesus' yoke is not a lax interpretation of Torah—quite the contrary! He teaches his disciples that merely keeping the law is not good enough; they must go further (Matt 5:21-48). If the law allows "an eye for an eye and a tooth for a tooth" (Lev 24:20), Jesus' disciples must instead try to short-circuit cycles of violence by taking nonviolent action that confronts evildoers, while praying for and loving such enemies (Matt 5:38-48).

Instead of being a restrictive and burdensome way to live, this teaching is freeing; it lightens burdens of oppression. This is the opposite of what some of the other religious leaders of Jesus' day do: "They tie up heavy burdens, hard to bear, and lay them on the shoulders of others; but they themselves are unwilling to lift a finger to move them" (Matt 23:4, NRSV). By contrast, disciples of Jesus are yoked with him and with one another, intent on lifting the weight born of injustice from the backs of those who are downtrodden.

The rest that is promised by Jesus echoes that bestowed on those who let themselves be yoked to Woman Wisdom's teaching (Sir 6:28). It also echoes that of the Creator (Gen 2:1-3), who rested in order to delight in the goodness of all that had been made, while setting creation free to flourish. Woman Wisdom, also present at creation (Prov 8:23-31), shares in this unbounded joy.

When believing communities gather to share Sabbath rest, we celebrate the divine delight in creation (Exod 20:8-11) and our participation in the recreative and liberating work of the Holy One, embodied in Jesus, who is Wisdom incarnate, intent on teaching the way that lifts heavy yokes.

PRAYING WITH SCRIPTURE

1. Allow Jesus to speak to you as Woman Wisdom. What do you hear?

2. Reflect on how Jesus' gift of rest is linked to taking up his yoke.

3. How is your faith community working to lift the yoke of injustice from those who are unjustly bound?

MYSTERIOUS GIFT

Fifteenth Sunday in Ordinary Time

Readings: Isa 55:10-11; Ps 65:10, 11, 12-13, 14;
Rom 8:18-23; Matt 13:1-23

*"Knowledge of the mysteries of the kingdom of heaven
has been granted to you"* (Matt 13:11)

The Pew Forum on Religion & Public Life reports that the fastest grow-ing religious denomination is "none." Among the 19.6 percent who do not identify themselves with any religion, approximately three-quarters had been affiliated with a religion as children. One in three young adults, ages eighteen to twenty-nine, claims no religious affiliation (*"Nones" on the Rise* [Washington, DC: Pew Research Center, 2012]). The study prompts impor-tant questions: Why is this happening, and what can be done about it? The Matthean community asked similar questions, as reflected in today's gospel. Why do some accept Jesus' interpretation of the law while others do not?

Like all Jesus' parables, the one in today's gospel is open to a variety of interpretations. If we take the sower as the focus, the parable invites us to reflect on the boundless generosity of God, who offers the Word, in the person of Jesus, to all in the hope of a fruitful response, no matter how poorly prepared to receive it some may seem to be. If we zero in on the seed, the parable assures us of the efficacy of the word. No matter what the yield, the seed itself is good, and it will bear fruit. If we take the harvest as the focus, the explosive return propels us into reflection on eschatological fulfillment of hopes beyond our wildest dreams. Finally, if the different types of soil are our focus, the parable urges effort to do everything possible to cull out obstacles and cultivate maximum receptivity to the word.

As Jesus' first followers struggled to understand why others did not respond as they did to Jesus' teaching, they turned to the prophet Isaiah. Isaiah articulates that this experience is repeated in the life of every prophet: some people are disposed to see and hear and respond positively to the prophet's message, while others close themselves off to the challenging word that could bring healing and that could free them to live life more fully in God's love. To explain the negative response by the latter, Isaiah puts the onus not on the prophet, nor on the message, but on those who deliberately close themselves off to the prophet's words and actions.

In the gospel, Jesus explains that the ability to accept his teaching is a gift from God. What is given is "knowledge of the mysteries of the kingdom of heaven" (v. 11). This is the only time that the word "mysteries" appears in the gospels (Matt 13:11 and parallels). In other Jewish sources the term "mystery" is associated with God's purposes for the end times (e.g., Dan 2:27-28; 1 Enoch 68:5; 4 Ezra 10:38). Here the "mystery" is the presence of God's realm in Jesus and his ministry.

While verses 11 and 12 explain that knowledge of the mysteries is God's gift, verses 13 to 17 emphasize human responsibility to cultivate receptivity so as to be able to respond as fully as possible to the gift. Some let the gift be snatched from them; some toss it aside in favor of something else that seems more alluring. Work must be done to root out whatever might stand in the way of allowing the gift to unfold all its riches. The parable and its allegorical interpretation undercut any smugness or complacency on the part of those who have received the gift. The gospel invites us to shift our focus from wondering whether the "seed" is effective—it is!—or why others' soil is unreceptive, to the question of how those who have received the gift can be intent on helping prepare receptive soil and to continue the profligate and indiscriminate work of the Divine Sower, who eagerly shares the mysteries far and wide.

PRAYING WITH SCRIPTURE

1. Ask the Divine Sower how you might share the word with someone who is not a churchgoer.

2. Let Jesus clear away the rocks and thorns in your soil.

3. Give thanks for the rich harvest produced in you.

WISDOM ABOUT WEEDS

Sixteenth Sunday in Ordinary Time

Readings: Wis 12:13, 16-19; Ps 86:5-6, 9-10, 15-16;
Rom 8:26-27; Matt 13:24-43

"Let them grow together until harvest" (Matt 13:30)

What is one to do when an enemy who has been the mastermind behind thousands of deaths is discovered hiding within the territory of a friendly nation? What to do when weeds are discovered sprouting among the good grain? Do you pull out the destructive intruders or let them grow? How did they get there?

Who or what were the "weeds" in the minds of Matthean Christians? Were they Gentiles who were infiltrating with their corrosive influences, like pesky, pungent mustard that violated the set boundaries and spread uncontrollably into well-defined Jewish fields? Were they evildoers in general or persecutors of the followers of Jesus, who, in the minds of the latter, should have been already permanently defeated now that the Messiah had come? Why is the evil one still exercising power?

Today's gospel opens myriad questions and gives helpful directions toward finding answers. The householder who sowed the good seed first acknowledges that the weeds are the work of an enemy, and takes the onus off the worried slaves who might have been blamed for not tending the field well or for sowing inferior seed. The parable focuses more on what to do than explaining how it happened.

One line of response proposed by the slaves is to pull up all the weeds immediately. The landowner decides against this course of action. Pulling up the weeds might uproot the wheat along with them. The separation can happen later, at the harvest time.

Is this a wise decision? Are the ones who actually work the land thinking that this absentee landlord doesn't know anything about farming? Will his approach be shown to be unrealistic when his wheat has been choked out by the weeds and when it proves impossible to sort out darnel from wheat by winnowing?

Authoritative voices in the early church agreed with the householder and urged forbearance toward sinners. Saint Augustine, for example, used this parable to argue that heretics or the lapsed should not be cut off from the church, contrary to the position of the Donatists. According to Hippolytus (*Haer*. 9.12.22) Bishop Callistus of Rome likewise interpreted "Let the tares grow along with the wheat" as "Let sinners remain in the church."

If the parable proper (vv. 24-30) reflects struggles of the early Christians to include as full participants Gentiles and other "sinners," the allegorical explanation (vv. 36-43) points outside the Christian community to "the world" (v. 38) as the ground of conflict. In these verses, the patient forbearance of the householder is gone as the end-time reapers throw all the evildoers into a fiery furnace. There is a distinct difference from the situation in verses 24-30. Now it is harvest time, a metaphor for end-time judgment, and the action is carried out by God's angels, not human beings. There is an implicit warning to us not to impetuously assume the role of the divine judge, who alone sorts out good from evil.

The nonretaliatory reproach of the householder who has been humiliated by his enemy can seem weak. When read with the parable of the leaven, it speaks instead of the womanly strength of God, whose transformative work is hidden in the agitating action of kneading the bread. With the first reading from Wisdom, it points to divine justice and might become manifest in leniency, clemency, and kindness. It is this paradoxical approach to rooting out evil, exemplified in Jesus' boundless forgiveness and inclusive table practices, that we are offered.

PRAYING WITH SCRIPTURE

1. Pray for the grace of forbearance.

2. Reflect on how goodness only grows through struggle with its opposite.

3. Let the Spirit's "groanings" (Rom 8:26) intercede through you when you do not know how to pray.

SURPRISED BY JOY

Seventeenth Sunday in Ordinary Time

Readings: 1 Kgs 3:5, 7-12; Ps 119:57, 72, 76-77, 127-128, 129-130 ; Rom 8:28-30; Matt 13:44-52

> *"[O]ut of joy [he] goes and sells all that he has and buys that field"* (Matt 13:44)

What would make you most happy? If given the chance, would you ask for an understanding heart, as Solomon did in today's first reading and which the disciples claim to have at the end of today's gospel? Is happiness something to be sought or does it find you? There is no end to "how-to" books and websites that tout surefire steps to achieve happiness. The American novelist Nathaniel Hawthorne (1804–64), however, reminds us that "happiness is a butterfly, which, when pursued, is always just beyond your grasp, but which, if you will sit down quietly, may alight upon you."

Today's gospel offers three short parables about how one attains not only happiness but the even deeper gift of lasting joy. In the first instance, a person unexpectedly finds buried treasure. Perhaps he is digging a well or a hole for a fence post, when suddenly he strikes a hoard of coins left behind by a previous owner who, for some reason, was unable to reclaim it. The digger is likely a poor peasant, a hired day laborer, at the bottom of the social scale. The parable emphasizes how overjoyed he is at this unexpected find that will change his life. With reckless abandon he sells all he has in order to acquire the field with its treasure.

The second parable takes us to the other end of the social spectrum. A merchant in search of fine pearls would have been a rich man, most likely making his money on the backs of the poor divers in his employ. Merchants are generally depicted negatively in the Scriptures (Sir 26:20; Isa 23:8; Ezek 27), as avaricious and corrupt. The surprise is that even such persons as this could come upon the reign of God and be moved to sell all they have for this pearl of great price.

If there is discomfort among the hearers of Jesus' parables that both a poor peasant and a rich merchant could be found in the reign of God, a third parable, about a net that pulls in all kinds of fish, asks disciples to suspend judgment about who is wicked and who is righteous, leaving the sorting to God's angels at the end of the age. There are many verbal and thematic similarities here to the parable of the weeds and wheat (Matt 13:24-30, 36-43). The parable is also evocative of the call of the first disciples to be fishers of people, for which they abandon all else (Matt 4:18-20).

There is an element of surprise in each parable, whether concerning the manner of finding or who is to be found in God's reign. A further surprise is that the resultant joy leads to giving up all else. It is a paradoxical path to happiness. When it finds you, any instinct to hoard this treasure evaporates; what surfaces instead is the desire to divest oneself of everything.

The metaphors of the treasure and pearl break down, however, when they imply that the reign of God can be bought and owned. The startling message Jesus preaches is that happiness in God's reign cannot be purchased in any way—not by good deeds, nor with any other commodity. Rather, it is an astonishing free gift, attainable by all. While it cannot be bought, it costs everything. The price is not paid out of obligation or guilt but is a totally free self-surrender to irresistible joy. This is an old story, not to be kept locked in a storeroom, but meant to be told anew, by each who has been set free by joy.

PRAYING WITH SCRIPTURE

1. Give thanks for the ways in which you have been surprised by joy.

2. What do you ask for as the Holy One offers to give you your heart's desire?

3. Ask the Spirit's help to let go of whatever stands in the way of your self-surrender to lasting joy.

NO MORE HUNGER

Eighteenth Sunday in Ordinary Time

Readings: Isa 55:1-3; Ps 145:8-9, 15-16, 17-18;
Rom 8:35, 37-39; Matt 14:13-21

"They all ate and were satisfied" (Matt 14:20)

No one really knows the precise number of hungry people in our world, but the United Nations Food and Agriculture Organization estimates it to be 925 million—that's approximately one of every seven people. The vast majority are in Asia and the Pacific (578 million), then sub-Saharan Africa (239 million), followed by Latin America and the Caribbean (53 million), then Northeast and North Africa (37 million), and some 19 million in developed countries. In 1996 the World Food Summit set out to reduce the number of malnourished people by half by 2015. Although there has been modest progress in some areas of the world, the number of hungry people has actually increased in the past decade and a half.

Hunger was no stranger in the days of Isaiah and of Jesus as well. In the first reading, Isaiah voices the dream of the returning exiles. With their pitiful resources, they long for all to be able to eat well, without having to pay a cent. No one would die of thirst or malnutrition. In the gospel, Jesus enacts God's promise to fill the hungry with good food, as he feeds a crowd of thousands. This is not only an act of heartfelt compassion, but it is also a politically subversive action. In Jesus' day, as now, food is about power. The rich who had control of land and the means of food production and distribution, who comprised about 2–3 percent of the people, were the ones who ate well and plentifully. The rest struggled daily to feed themselves and their children. Taxes, pestilence, and drought often ate up their reserves and left them at the brink of starvation.

In today's world, there is easily enough food for everyone, and then some. But not all have enough land to grow food or sufficient income to purchase it. In the gospel, Jesus' disciples presume that there is enough food for everyone, but they figure it is someone else's responsibility to provide it. They want to send everyone off to buy their own food, thinking that everyone has money and that the surrounding villages have the resources to feed the multitude. Jesus directs them away from an impulse toward self-sufficiency to a solution that depends on remaining in community and pooling and redistributing their resources. In a eucharistic action, he transforms all that they have, and there is enough.

At the end of the episode, Matthew's notice that the count of five thousand did not include the women and children is a reminder that children and their mothers are the ones who are hardest hit by hunger. Even when women make sure their husbands and children are fed before they themselves eat, some five million children die every year because of undernutrition.

The gospel today invites us to resist the temptation to consider it someone else's responsibility to address the problem of world hunger. When we gather at Eucharist, we not only give thanks for God's gifts received freely and abundantly, but together we seek to understand the causes of hunger and redouble our efforts to galvanize the church's energies toward aiding peoples and nations to take the drastic measures needed.

The opening verses of today's gospel remind us that such actions provoke opposition from those who benefit from the unequal distribution. On the heels of the execution of John, Jesus fed the crowds, knowing he could be the next victim of Rome. Was it because he was counting the women and children who would otherwise perish?

PRAYING WITH SCRIPTURE

1. How do our eucharistic celebrations impel us to act for just global food distribution?

2. Ask Jesus to share his compassionate heart with you.

3. Ask the Spirit to show you how to make the concerns of women and children central.

A SOUND OF SHEER SILENCE

──────── **Nineteenth Sunday in Ordinary Time**

Readings: 1 Kgs 19:9a, 11-13a; Ps 85:9, 10, 11-12, 13-14;
Rom 9:1-5; Matt 14:22-33

"After the fire [there was] a sound of sheer silence . . ."
(1 Kgs 19:12, NRSV)

At the conclusion of a recent performance of the symphony, a few seconds elapsed before the audience burst into applause. During the ensuing intermission, a handful of patrons remained and sat still, quietly relishing the exquisite sounds they had just heard. The majority, however, had quickly whipped out their cell phones and were checking messages, texting, and talking. The need for constant communication won out over the momentary gift of contemplative silence. Today's readings invite us to choose to enter into spaces of silence, where it is easier to hear the One who is constantly communicating divine love to us.

In the first reading, Elijah is discouraged and afraid for his life. He has fled from the deadly intentions of Jezebel into the desert, and has plopped himself under a broom tree and asked God to let him die. God has other plans, however, and an angel provides him with food and drink. Twice the angel has to urge him to eat and drink. He finally does so and is thus fortified for his forty-day trek to Mount Horeb, also called Sinai. At this same mountain, God had been revealed to Moses, who likewise stood in a cleft in the rock as God's glory passed by (Exod 33:21).

At a time of deep fear and distress, Elijah goes to the place that connects him again with the roots of Israel's covenantal bond with the Holy One. But God is not manifest in devouring fire, like that which surrounded the mountain at the giving of the law to Moses (Exod 24:17). Nor can Elijah hear God in the fierce, crushing wind or in the earthquake. It is in "a sound of sheer silence" (so NRSV; the Lectionary [NAB] translates *qôl děmāmāh dăqqāh* to "a tiny whispering sound") that Elijah hears the voice of God.

"What are you doing here, Elijah?" (1 Kgs 19:13, NRSV) is the probing question that invites Elijah and us to reflect on whether our actions and choices are leading us to fulfill our hearts' deepest desires for oneness with God and God's purposes. The subsequent verses sketch out how God strengthens Elijah for the remainder of his prophetic mission before he dies.

In the gospel, we see Jesus likewise retreat to a mountain by himself to pray, following the noisiness of healing and feeding a crowd of more than five thousand people. That previous episode begins with the note that Jesus had just heard of the death of John the Baptist and had withdrawn to a deserted place by himself (Matt 14:13). But the crowds find him and he breaks out of his solitude to respond compassionately to their needs.

Today's gospel begins with Jesus' effort to retreat again. Even at night, the peoples' need for him does not abate. His disciples have been in distress in their boat on the lake ever since he left them at evening. He does not go to them immediately, however, but waits until the fourth watch of the night, the last watch, about three hours before dawn. We can surmise that although he is aware of the strong wind that is tossing them about, he remains in solitude, in the necessary inner stillness, where he experiences oneness with God, and becomes strengthened to continue to minister compassionately.

Coming to the disciples at last, he shares with them his gift of fearlessness. Although his beloved mentor has been executed, and although he can see a similar fate awaiting him as well, from the still center of his heart set on God, he can do what seems impossible. Disciples, too, when they grasp his outstretched hand to come to him, find in him the still center, where his contagious courage dispels all fear.

PRAYING WITH SCRIPTURE

1. Where is the mountain where you can hear God's voice in the sheer silence?

2. Ask Jesus to help you know when to put aside urgent demands so you can seek solitude for prayer.

3. Give thanks for the times you have been fearless in stepping out into roiling waters by taking Jesus' hand.

DOGGED FAITH

Twentieth Sunday in Ordinary Time

Readings: Isa 56:1, 6-7; Ps 67:2-3, 5, 6, 8;
Rom 11:13-15, 29-32; Matt 15:21-28

"[E]ven the dogs eat the scraps
that fall from the table of their masters" (Matt 15:27)

They call themselves the "Brain Tumor Moms." Three mothers in Massachusetts banded together after receiving the heartbreaking news that their young daughters have brain cancer. Bent on advancing progress beyond outdated pediatric brain research, in 2009 alone they raised $250,000 for the Dana-Farber Cancer Institute by walking, pleading, and repeated asking, despite frequent rebuffs.

In today's gospel, there is an equally determined mother who pleads with Jesus to heal her daughter. It happens in the region of Tyre and Sidon. It is puzzling that he should go there, since the Matthean Jesus is intent on ministering only to the lost sheep of the house of Israel (Matt 10:6). Matthew has just recounted the execution of John the Baptist, preceded by the ominous notice that Jesus has also come to Herod's attention (Matt 14:1-12). Most likely, Jesus goes to the coastal cities to get out of Herod's jurisdiction and to lie low for a time. He needs time to grieve over his beloved teacher and relative. He can be anonymous in Tyre and Sidon and can regroup and strategize about when and how to continue his mission publicly.

But he is recognized. A Canaanite woman comes pleading for her daughter. By labeling the woman with the outmoded term "Canaanite," Matthew makes her the archetypal enemy; one of those with whom Israel struggled for possession of the land. Oddly, this so-called enemy knows both the right Jewish prayer formulas and the proper messianic title for Jesus. Her impassioned plea, *kyrie eleēson,* "Have mercy on me, Lord," echoes Psalm 109:26 as well as the pleas of the blind men (Matt 9:27; 20:30, 31) and the father of the boy with epilepsy (Matt 17:15). In those instances, Jesus quickly heals.

To the woman he makes no response at all. Never before has Jesus ignored someone who pleaded with him for compassion. The disciples also urge him to send her away. When he finally speaks with her, he insists he has nothing for her and that his mission is only to his own people.

If the woman were seeking healing for herself, she might have given up, but there is nothing that fuels a mother's audacity more than her child's well-being. She kneels before Jesus, a gesture of homage, but in so doing she also blocks his way, insisting that he act on her behalf. This time Jesus' response is terribly insulting: "It is not right to take the food of the children and throw it to the dogs." Some biblical scholars try to tone down the insult, understanding it as an endearing address to a pet. Others think Jesus is reciting a common saying of his day that reflected animosity of Galileans toward the people on the coast, to whom their wheat would be exported, even in times of shortage (see 1 Kgs 5:11; Acts 12:20). Whatever the genesis of Jesus' comment, calling the woman a dog is a gross insult.

Rather than turn away or return insult for insult, the mother redirects her rage, finding clever words, and remaining respectful toward Jesus: "Please, Lord, for even the dogs eat the scraps that fall from the table of their masters." With that, something shifts in Jesus. The woman stretches him to see her not as "other," or as "enemy," but as one of his own, one with whom he shares a common humanity, a common faith in God, a common desire for the well-being of children. He recognizes her great faith, having often chided his disciples for their "little faith" (Matt 6:30; 8:26; 14:31; 16:8; 17:20). Beyond securing the healing of her daughter, the narrative depicts this woman sparking in Jesus the idea that his mission is for all people, a notion that will be fanned into flame by those who carry on his mission after his death (Matt 28:19).

PRAYING WITH SCRIPTURE

1. Pray for the wisdom to know how best to advocate for women, children, and the most vulnerable.

2. Pray for the grace to stand firm and speak truth respectfully, even when insulted or ignored.

3. Pray for the grace to act with inclusive love, from which no one is excluded.

WHO DO YOU SAY YOU ARE?

Twenty-First Sunday in Ordinary Time

Readings: Isa 22:19-23; Ps 138:1-2, 2-3, 6, 8;
Rom 11:33-36; Matt 16:13-20

"Who do you say that I am?" (Matt 16:15)

The question Jesus poses in today's gospel is not a pop quiz for the disciples. Since it comes halfway through Matthew's Gospel, at a critical turning point, we might be tempted to think Jesus is giving a kind of midterm exam to see how well the disciples are understanding him and to test whether they have what it takes to go the rest of the journey with him. But, the scene may also reflect Jesus' own development in understanding his identity and mission. Taking Jesus' humanity seriously, and recalling Luke's assertion that "Jesus increased in wisdom and in years, and in divine and human favor" (Luke 2:52, NRSV), we might say that in today's gospel and next Sunday's, we see a glimpse of Jesus' deepening understanding of what it meant to be "the Christ, the Son of the living God" (v. 16).

In contrast to modern Western cultures in which an individual expends energy trying to find a unique identity as a person distinct from other persons, in Jesus' culture, characterized by dyadic personality, a person understood himself or herself only in relationship to the groups in which she or he was embedded: family, clan, nation, and religion. Paul, for example, identifies himself as "a member of the people of Israel, of the tribe of Benjamin, a Hebrew born of Hebrews; as to the law, a Pharisee" (Phil 3:5, NRSV). Earlier in the gospel, the people of Jesus' hometown identify him as "the carpenter's son," whose mother is Mary, and whose brothers are James, Joseph, Simon, Judas, and who also has sisters (Matt 13:55-56). In addition, in such a culture, the perceptions of others also help to shape a person's identity.

In today's gospel, Jesus seeks out others' perceptions as he solidifies his understanding of himself. The disciples first report that people align Jesus with revered prophetic figures: John the Baptist, Elijah, Jeremiah. While there are many parallels between Jesus and these prophets, Matthew clearly distinguishes Jesus from them. He is the "more powerful" one "coming after" John (Matt 3:11, NRSV). And it is John who embodies the returned Elijah (Matt 11:14; 17:12).

As Jesus presses the disciples for their own response, Peter, the spokesperson for the group, rightly declares, "You are the Messiah [*christos*]" (Matt 16:16, NRSV). This is a term used in the Old Testament for one who is set apart by God for particular service, such as kings (Ps 2:2; 89:20), priests (Lev 4:3, 5), and prophets (1 Kgs 19:16). That Jesus is *christos*, "anointed," is not a new revelation in Matthew's Gospel (see 1:1, 17, 18; 11:2). But the nature of Jesus' messiahship as entailing suffering and death is articulated for the first time in the ensuing verses (16:21-27), the gospel for next Sunday.

As Jesus' identity emerges and solidifies, so too does that of Peter. Verses 17 to 19 are unique to Matthew, with a wordplay on the name *Petros*, "rock," in Greek. Jesus exalts the emerging rocklike faith of Peter and of the whole community of disciples whose identity is tied up in that of Jesus. Yet in the very next verses, the "rock" will falter when confronted with the stumbling block (*scandalon*, 18:6, 7) of Jesus' passion. Nonetheless, as the gospel progresses, Jesus continues to call him "Peter," enabling him to become what he is named. Just as the disciples' naming of Jesus as "Messiah" and partnering with him in his messianic mission enabled him to embrace all that being the "anointed" one entailed, so too Jesus' identification of the believing community as "rock solid" brought forth that quality in them. Likewise, we are invited to let Jesus and our faith community call forth our deepest identity as followers of the anointed, whose solidity is sure.

PRAYING WITH SCRIPTURE

1. What is Jesus saying to you about your identity as his follower?

2. How are your gifts for mission identified by your faith community?

3. Who do you say you are?

FINDING YOUR SELF

Twenty-Second Sunday in Ordinary Time

Readings: Jer 20:7-9; Ps 63:2, 3-4, 5-6, 8-9;
Rom 12:1-2; Matt 16:21-27

"If any want to become my followers,
let them deny themselves and
take up their cross and follow me" (Matt 16:24, NRSV)

Having had the privilege some years ago to listen to indigenous women in La Paz, Bolivia, reflect on today's gospel, I can never hear it without remembering their interpretation: "We women identify strongly with the crucified Christ and his sufferings. There is a strong sense of submission in our Aymara and Quechua cultures. Women submit to sexual abuse from their fathers, uncles, and husbands, with a strong sense of resignation, thinking that whatever suffering they endure, they do silently and hero-ically, as their way of carrying the cross with Jesus" (quoted in Barbara E. Reid, *Taking Up the Cross: New Testament Interpretations Through Latina and Feminist Eyes* [Minneapolis: Fortress Press, 2007], 22).

This particular group had come through a process of learning to interpret the gospel differently, so that their consciousness of themselves as lovable and precious in God's eyes had been heightened; and thereafter they ques-tioned the wisdom they had received for generations about how submitting to abuse and injustice was the way to identify with the crucified Christ. Gradually, they tested out new ways of relating, as they claimed their power, uniting with one another to bring about change for themselves and their daughters.

What these women came to discover was the way in which a misreading of today's gospel had obliterated their sense of self and had kept them cowering in abusive relationships. How could Jesus, who was so intent on lifting up those who were bowed down and on healing all who suffered, have meant it otherwise for them, they reasoned.

One does not have to go to Bolivia to find abuse justified by such interpretations of the cross. Whether immediately visible or not, such situations can be found in almost every community. A closer look at the context of Jesus' saying reveals that he is speaking about a particular kind of suffering that his disciples must be willing to embrace: that which comes as a direct result of following his manner of life and mission. Suffering that comes from abuse and injustice is to be resisted and eradicated to the extent possible, as Jesus did throughout his ministry.

Moreover, the saying about denial of self is not referring to giving up certain pleasures, like forgoing chocolate during Lent. Rather, it refers to a disciple's choice to lose oneself entirely in Christ—to take on Christ's way of life and mission and his very identity as one's own. This identity does not center on suffering, but on the love of God, expressed through loving service to one another, intent on bringing forth life to the full for all. But not all will welcome such a manner of living and loving that undermines systems of domination and submission. The repercussions one is willing to risk for the sake of living and proclaiming the gospel—that is the cross.

For these women in La Paz, a newfound understanding of the gospel was born in meetings in which they were able to join in solidarity to share their experiences and to reflect together with new eyes on the Scriptures. From this grew their sense of being empowered, beloved by God, and able to choose to band together to confront and end the suffering they and others they loved were experiencing.

True to today's gospel, these women indeed found their lives. As Jesus increasingly came to understand what lay ahead for him from his own denial of self in finding his true life, Peter became all the more resistant and fearful. How do you find yourself?

PRAYING WITH SCRIPTURE

1. What does "taking up the cross" mean in your life?

2. Do you stumble at the thought of losing yourself in order to find yourself in Christ?

3. Ask Jesus to show you how to overcome the fear of repercussions for living and spreading his liberating love.

A RECIPE FOR RECONCILIATION

Twenty-Third Sunday in Ordinary Time

Readings: Ezek 33:7-9; Ps 95:1-2, 6-7, 8-9;
Rom 13:8-10; Matt 18:15-20

"[I]f two of you agree on earth
about anything for which they are to pray,
it shall be granted to them" (Matt 18:19)

Some years ago one of the sisters with whom I lived overheard a very
hurtful comment made about her by one of her coworkers. For weeks, the
rest of us heard her replay the remark again and again, and her hurt feel-
ings grew exponentially. Finally, we urged her to go speak with the person
who had offended her to try to smooth things out. After a pause, she con-
fessed, "I think I'd rather have my grievance!"

In today's gospel, Jesus provides advice to his disciples on how to move
step-by-step toward reconciling grievances within the Christian community.
This is not a recipe that can be applied to all situations, but it gives some
specific advice on how to resolve differences when one is hurt by another
member of the community.

First of all, the initiative almost always comes from the one who has been
aggrieved. Hardly ever do reconciliation processes begin with those who
have done the harm coming to their senses and asking forgiveness. The
first step, says Jesus, is for the one who has suffered the hurt to confront
the person who has inflicted it. This is not as easy as it may sound. As my
sister found, we often relish retelling the story to others, while being reluc-
tant to speak directly to the one who has hurt us. But there will never be
peace as long as the one harmed allows the hurt to fester and grow by
holding on to it and recounting it to others. If, however, the one hurt musters
the courage to speak to the other, and if the other has the courage to listen
honestly and openly, reconciliation becomes a possibility.

What Jesus does not outline here is that for true reconciliation to occur, the one who is hurt must be willing to offer forgiveness, and the perpetrator of the harm must be willing to acknowledge it truthfully, amend the behavior, and make restitution, if possible. Then there is the possibility of a new future of peaceable interrelation between the two.

What if one-on-one confrontation does not work? Then, Jesus says, take one or two others along with you. This is not so that you can gang up on the one who hurt you but rather for establishing the truth of what happened. In Jewish tradition, two witnesses are needed for verification. Or, to use today's language, an impartial mediator or two can help establish the truth and can help bring the parties to an agreement.

Jesus anticipates that the disciples will press him further: But what if that doesn't work either? Then, Jesus says, involve the whole community, since any rupture in relationships within the Christian community affects all the members. Note that in verse 18 the whole community has a role in binding and loosing offenses (cf. Matt 16:19). If this strategy fails as well, Jesus then says to treat the offender as "a Gentile or a tax collector."

At first this may seem to mean that the offender should be excluded from the community. But when we look at the way Jesus befriended and ate with such people (see Matt 8:5-13; 9:9-13; 11:19;15:21-28), it may be that Jesus is asking us to be willing to sit and break bread together, even when we have irreconcilable differences. It is important to note that the gospel text does not indicate the nature of the offense. The strategy outlined in today's gospel would not work for every kind of offense.

Finally, Jesus urges the community to pray together for reconciliation. Already the animosity melts away when parties to a grievance can agree to pray for resolution. When they can genuinely pray for good for the other, their prayer is already granted.

PRAYING WITH SCRIPTURE

1. Pray for the grace to start a process of reconciliation with someone who has offended you.

2. Ask Jesus to give you a listening ear to be able to repent of ways you have offended others.

3. Has your faith community made a commitment to pray intentionally for peace?

ENDLESS FORGIVENESS

Twenty-Fourth Sunday in Ordinary Time

Readings: Sir 27:30–28:7; Ps 103:1-2, 3-4, 9-10, 11-12;
Rom 14:7-9; Matt 18:21-35

"[H]ow often must I forgive?" (Matt 18:21)

A survivor of domestic violence trusted me with her story and how she struggled with today's gospel. She felt she could not forgive her husband for his abuse toward her: "As a Catholic, I felt I had a moral responsibility and obligation to forgive [him] for his violence at the moment he was about to murder me. I believed I had to imitate Jesus' final act of love during his crucifixion. I worried that rather than feeling forgiveness I might feel hatred in my heart and that my last words would be to condemn [him] to hell for all eternity. I feared that if I failed to forgive him completely before I died, then I might end up in hell myself" (Margaret M. Leddy, "Domestic Violence: A Pastoral Response Guide" [M.A.P.S. thesis, Catholic Theological Union, Chicago, 2004], 10).

There is a dangerous side to Jesus' teaching to forgive endless numbers of times. What happens when we are not yet able to forgive? What happens when the offer of forgiveness is not met with repentance and restitution on the part of the offender? There are times, as in cases of domestic violence, when endless forgiveness fuels the cycle of abuse, and does not bring peace and reconciliation. Processes of forgiveness and reconciliation are complex and cannot be reduced to simple formulas.

Today's gospel is a continuation of last week's, where Jesus outlines a process for initiating reconciliation when there are ruptures within the Christian community. He speaks about moving from one-on-one confrontation to mediation to involvement of the whole community. It is in response to this that Peter asks how often one must forgive. He rightly recognizes the difficulties and complications that accompany such processes. Jesus' response is that there is no limit to the number of times one must try to forgive. There are endless hurts that require endless offers of forgiveness and endless acts of repentance. One must always be ready to do the difficult work of repairing and reconciling.

In the ensuing parable about the servant who is forgiven a great debt, Jesus shifts the emphasis away from the burden and the difficulty of the work of reconciliation, as he calls attention to the utter gratuity of the gift of forgiveness. The only way to respond adequately to such a gift is to pay it forward. The servant can never repay the king, but he can act in the same forgiving manner to those indebted to him. But, as the second act of the parable unfolds, we find him doing the exact opposite. Then, in a disturbing turn of events, the king retracts his forgiveness. Most troubling is that this is likened to God's reneging on forgiveness if we do not forgive from the heart. This verse recalls the ending of the prayer that Jesus teaches his disciples: "Forgive us our debts, as we also have forgiven our debtors" (Matt 6:12, NRSV), with the added admonition that our ability to offer forgiveness is intimately related to our ability to receive it (6:14-15).

The point is not that God is fickle about forgiveness, taking it back if we do not do likewise, nor that God is vindictive if we fail to follow the divine lead. Rather, the parable is a stark warning of the consequences of letting our hearts become solidified in unforgiveness. A heart hardened in revenge sets in motion endless cycles of violence. The parable exposes the way that our choice to forgive (or not) redounds upon us. If we try to forgive and pray for the ability to forgive even when we are not yet able to, we open ourselves all the more to the experience of God's tender mercy toward us, enabling us to extend that mercy and compassion toward others. Nothing we can do can take divine forgiveness away from us, but we can do things that hinder its powerful effect on us.

PRAYING WITH SCRIPTURE

1. Pray for the ability to forgive whatever seems unforgivable.

2. Ask Jesus to open your heart even more fully to divine compassion.

3. Pray for the wisdom to know when to leave an abusive situation when offers of forgiveness are not matched by repentance by the perpetrator.

JUSTICE IN THE REIGN OF GOD

Twenty-Fifth Sunday in Ordinary Time

Readings: Isa 55:6-9; Ps 145:2-3, 8-9, 17-18;
Phil 1:20c-24, 27a; Matt 20:1-16a

"Friend, I am doing you no wrong" (Matt 20:13, NRSV)

The parable in today's gospel seems so unfair. Don't people who work longer and harder deserve more pay? How can it be just that the vineyard owner pays all the laborers the same when they haven't worked the same amount of time?

These troublesome questions arise when we stand in the place of those who were hired first and who worked the whole long day in the sun.

It was at my grandfather's funeral that I first heard an interpretation of this parable that made sense to me. The priest spoke about how my grandfather, who converted to Catholicism on his deathbed, was like those who were hired last in the parable. He talked about how some people, when they are going on a train trip, buy their tickets far in advance, ensuring their reserved seat. Others rush into the station at the very last moment, buy their ticket, and reach the same destination at the same time as those who planned ahead. The assurance that my grandpa had arrived at the same heavenly destination that all of us were striving for was very comforting to me as a youngster.

I thought the key for those first hired was to try to love the ones who got in just under the wire. But how to foster that love for everyone was a question that still stumped me.

A woman at a Bible study workshop many years later helped me understand this parable from a whole other angle. She was a single mother, raising three children alone after her husband deserted them. She had little education, and few marketable skills. Day after day she stood in line at the unemployment office, hoping against hope for a job.

As she read the parable, she remarked that the ones standing idle all day long in the marketplace were not lazy. They would gladly work if anyone would hire them. But they were always left behind because they were old, infirm, and unskilled, unable to work as hard as the more robust. They were like her and the people who thronged to the unemployment lines these days, she said.

As she reflected on the ending of the parable, she observed that if the landowner had given the laborers that were hired last anything other than one day's wage, what good would that do? How would they feed their children? Sure, she admitted, the first hired had worked all day in the hot sun, but they also had the satisfaction of knowing all day long that at the end of the day they would be able to feed their families.

Justice, in God's reign, she proposed, is about everybody being able to eat at the end of the day, no matter what each one's capacity to work. God's justice, she advanced, cannot be earned and does not depend on how much you work.

This explanation seems to be much closer to what Jesus' original audience of people struggling to survive would have understood. The assertion of the vineyard owner that he is doing no injustice to the earlier hired workers challenges those in privileged positions to examine their sense of entitlement. Does it take anything away from the first hired if the last hired receive the same wage?

The vineyard owner's question in verse 15 points out the destructiveness of evil-eye envy in a community. The owner asks, literally, "Is your eye evil (*ponēros*) because I am good (*agathos*)?" The question is about God's goodness, which is extended equally to all, and how difficult it is for us not to look enviously on goodness poured out on others, even as it has been lavished upon ourselves. Is it not, however, a great relief that God's justice does not mean that people get what they deserve?

PRAYING WITH SCRIPTURE

1. What does this parable say to us about treatment of immigrants and migrant laborers?

2. Pray to be able to look with the eyes of God, desiring good for all persons.

3. Reflect on how there are no degrees of salvation; in the eternal vineyard, all receive the full reward.

SAYING AND DOING

"Which of the two did his father's will?" (Matt 21:31)

Unlike other parables, the one in today's gospel does not seem to pose a difficult riddle. A father asks each of his two sons to go out to work in the vineyard. The first says no, but then changes his mind and goes. The second says yes, but does not follow through. It doesn't seem hard to answer Jesus' question, "Which of the two did his father's will?" Isn't it the one who thought better of his original answer and actually complied with the father's command?

Not so, says another ancient version of this parable. In some early manuscripts of the gospel, the answer is that the second son did his father's will! In a culture where saving face is highly prized, it is deemed better to be publicly honored with an obedient response and privately shamed when the action does not follow, rather than be publicly shamed and privately honored.

In the literary context of Matthew's Gospel, Jesus directs this parable at the religious leaders who have tried to shame and discredit him publicly by challenging his authority. Jesus uses a technique similar to that of the prophet Nathan, who confronted King David about his sin with Bathsheba by telling a story about a rich man who took the one precious lamb of a poor man (2 Sam 12:1-12). Nathan invited David to pronounce judgment on a hypothetical situation, which ended up being a pronouncement on himself.

In similar fashion, Jesus' parable is designed to jar the religious leaders into conversion, so that there is coherence between what they say and teach, and what they do. Earlier, Jesus had warned disciples that merely saying "Lord, Lord" was not sufficient; they must also do the will of God (7:21-27).

In Matthew 23:3, Jesus warns the crowds and his disciples not to follow the example of the scribes and the Pharisees, because they do not practice what they preach. Today's gospel holds out hope to the religious leaders: there is still time to turn around and make their deeds match their words.

A startling statement at the conclusion of the parable is meant to jolt the leaders into a change of heart: tax collectors and prostitutes are entering the reign of God ahead of them. This saying does not refer to the actual makeup of the retinue of Jesus' disciples. Rather, it is a hyperbole meant to contrast the best and the worst imaginable. The point is that the religious leaders who should be the ones leading others into God's reign are not, while those who are thought least able to do so are repenting and believing and entering the reign of God.

It is always easier to see the discrepancies between saying and doing in someone else's behavior. I can smugly point a finger at the Pharisees in the gospel, or at other contemporary leaders, and see their need to change. It is harder to see the lack of a match between my own words and deeds. It is easy to say yes to following Jesus, but how difficult it is to do what that demands of us. If I say I value prayer, for example, do I actually carve out a consistent time and place to do it? If I say I am concerned for those who are poor, how is that visible in my lifestyle choices?

Fortunately, the burden of arriving at consistency in word and deed does not fall on our shoulders alone. Christ's "yes" to the self-emptying love described so eloquently by Paul in today's second reading is the empowering force that allows us not only to say yes, but also to do the corresponding deeds. Each day Christ's "yes" is pronounced anew in us, giving us myriad opportunities to open ourselves to conversion of heart and let those we regard least likely to do so to show us the way to enter God's reign.

PRAYING WITH SCRIPTURE

1. To what have you said yes? How is that visible in your actions?

2. To what has your faith community said yes? How is that visible in your collective actions?

3. What does Christ's self-emptying "yes" ask of you now?

OTHER TENANTS

Twenty-Seventh Sunday in Ordinary Time

Readings: Isa 5:1-7; Ps 80:9, 12, 13-14, 15-16, 19-20;
Phil 4:6-9; Matt 21:33-43

"What will the owner of the vineyard do?" (Matt 21:40)

Since December 2010, there have been an amazing number of uprisings, demonstrations, and protests in Arab countries, some of which have led to a change in leadership. Some have been relatively peaceful, accomplishing regime change with little bloodshed. Others have been brutal and bloody, costing many lives. There are some similarities between these contemporary movements and the situation that is described in today's gospel, which can be read as a peasant uprising against an oppressive landowner.

Weary of their landlessness and powerlessness, the tenants do away with all the landowner's envoys and even his son, the heir apparent, hoping to gain control of the land themselves. Verse 40 then poses a critical question: What, then, will the owner of the vineyard do? The response is swift and brutal: violence breeds even more violence, and the tenants will be put to a miserable death. One way in which this parable can be read is as a commentary on the futility of violence to accomplish change in ownership and leadership.

A more traditional reading of this parable is that it is an allegory, in which the vineyard represents Israel, the tenants are Israel's leaders, the vineyard owner is God, the messengers are the prophets, the son is Jesus. There are also clear allusions to a familiar parable from the prophet Isaiah, which we hear in the first reading. But there is a decided difference in the endings of the two parables. In Isaiah, when the vineyard owner is disappointed in the lack of fruit, he destroys the vineyard. In Jesus' parable, the vineyard is not destroyed, but rather entrusted to new leaders. In both parables, a focal point is the necessity of bearing fruit and the inability of the current leadership to cultivate the desired fruit. An additional twist is that if the parable is an allegory of salvation history, the inheritance that God's people long to claim is a free gift of the son; it need not be wrested from the owner. If the vineyard owner is God, would the response even to the death of the son not be forbearance, loving kindness, and extending one more opportunity for repentance, rather than violent destruction?

In the context of Matthew's Gospel, the parable is aimed at the religious leaders that oppose Jesus, and it points toward the necessity of new leadership. Some interpret the "others" to whom the vineyard is entrusted as the Gentile church that "supplants" Israel. This interpretation should be firmly rejected. In the gospel narrative, the change envisioned is from Jewish leaders who oppose Jesus to Jews who follow him. By Matthew's time Jesus' disciples, predominantly Jewish Christians, understood themselves as the "new tenants," even as they struggled to define themselves in relationship to their sibling, Pharisaic Judaism.

The parable poses a searing question regarding leadership of any organization, institution, or nation. If the leaders are not cultivating the fruitfulness of all members, then the leadership must be entrusted to others who will do so. Within the literary context of the gospel, hope is held out that current leaders could repent and become fruit-bearers and cultivators of fruitfulness in others. But the parable also notes that vintage time is near—code language for the eschatological time—the moment at which time to change runs out, and the decisions made all along have a finality. The gospel invites us to insist on having leaders who can cultivate fruitful abundance for all and to pursue nonviolent means of bringing about change in leadership when that is needed.

PRAYING WITH SCRIPTURE

1. How is the Spirit leading you to greater fruitfulness?

2. Pray to the Spirit for guidance in trying new kinds of leadership in your faith community.

3. How do you call forth the fruitful gifts of others?

DRESSED FOR THE FEAST

Twenty-Eighth Sunday in Ordinary Time

Readings: Isa 25:6-10a; Ps 23:1-3a, 3b-4, 5, 6;
Phil 4:12-14, 19-20; Matt 22:1-10

"[E]verything is ready; come to the feast" (Matt 22:4)

Two different kinds of invitations came to me in the mail this week. One came by postal service. The paper was of rich stock, and the lettering was exquisitely embossed. It was addressed by hand with elegant flourishes. A stamped envelope was included for the RSVP. The other came electronically, as an e-vite, sent to a vast list of friends and acquaintances. The invitation encouraged the recipients to spread the word to others. No response was necessary—one could just come and bring a dish to pass.

In today's gospel, the host of the great banquet seems to have used the ancient equivalents of both these kinds of invitations as he prepared for the wedding of his son. When those who had received formal invitations are summoned to the feast, they refused to come, even after two attempts by the servants. The king then instructs the servants to go out to the streets and invite everyone they find. They do so, gathering in the "bad and good alike," and the banquet hall is filled.

Matthew's version of the parable does not highlight the status divisions between the first and the last invited. Nor are the latter said to be poor, crippled, blind, and lame, as in Luke's version (14:15-24). Matthew does not elaborate on the excuses that the first invited gave, nor does he mention the necessity to compel the second tier of invitees. Instead, Matthew focuses on the profligacy of the host and the expected responses.

This is the third in a series of three parables directed at the religious leaders, who would be expected to be the first to receive and respond affirmatively to God's invitation through Jesus. But these are not the ones who fill the banquet hall. Jesus, as Woman Wisdom incarnate, calls out to all "from the highest places in the town," extending an e-vite to any who are willing to "walk in the way of insight" (Prov 9:3, 6, NRSV).

But there is a catch. One must come properly attired. In the Pauline letters we find frequent use of the metaphor of putting on clothing to signify the way of life one embraces. The Colossians are exhorted, "As God's chosen ones, holy and beloved, clothe yourselves with compassion, kindness, humility, meekness, and patience" (Col 3:12, NRSV; see also Rom 13:14; Gal 3:37). Likewise, Matthew would have all the guests clothe themselves with good deeds and faithfulness, ever ready for the banquet. More is needed than just showing up.

The Matthean version of this parable veers away from parabolic form, as it becomes a highly allegorized sketch of salvation history. While the extravagant generosity of the king in opening the banquet hall to all is a most apt depiction of God's invitation to us through Jesus, the vicious retaliation against those who killed the king's servants and the burning of the city are not depicting God's doings; they are allusions to the killing of servants like John the Baptist by Herod, and the destruction of Jerusalem in 70 CE by the Romans.

As in other Matthean parables, where unresponsive characters are "thrown into the outer darkness, where there will be weeping and gnashing of teeth" (Matt 8:12, NRSV; cf. 13:42, 50; 24:51; 25:30), there is a warning that refusal of the divine invitation has dire consequences. God does not inflict fiery punishment, but those who ignore God's invitation and do not allow themselves to be clothed in the garment of Jesus' ways of love, forgiveness, inclusivity, and nonviolent action for justice, choose for themselves a place at the table of retaliatory violence and destruction.

PRAYING WITH SCRIPTURE

1. Sit at the table of Woman Wisdom and ask her to feed you with insight and understanding.

2. As you approach the eucharistic table, pray that Christ will clothe you with the proper attire for his eternal feast.

3. Pray for one new piece of spiritual "clothing" each day this week.

TO PAY OR NOT TO PAY

Twenty-Ninth Sunday in Ordinary Time

Readings: Isa 45:1, 4-6; Ps 96:1, 3, 4-5, 7-8, 9-10;
1 Thess 1:1-5b; Matt 22:15-21

*"Then repay to Caesar what belongs to Caesar
and to God what belongs to God"* (Matt 22:21)

The Pharisees and Herodians in today's gospel, who pose the question to Jesus about paying tax to Caesar, are not seeking guidance in making a difficult moral decision. They are trying to trap Jesus into a no-win situation with a sticky question that has no easy solution. Since the Roman occupation of Palestine in 63 BCE, Jews were obliged to a census tax, or head tax, on each man, woman, and slave. The amount was one denarius (one day's pay) per year, and was to be paid with Roman coins, which in Jesus' day bore the image of the emperor Tiberius, who reigned from 14 to 37 CE.

The attitudes of Jesus' fellow Jews toward the Romans varied as did their strategies for resistance to the occupiers. Some resigned themselves to do what was necessary in order to live peaceably and dutifully paid their taxes, even while harboring resentment. Some paid the tax because they regarded the Romans as representing God's authority (see Rom 13:1-7; 1 Pet 2:13-17). Some, like the Herodians, derived their power from the Romans, and would have openly advocated paying tribute to Rome. Others were pushed to desperate straits by the exorbitant taxes levied on them and feared losing their land or falling so far into debt that they would be sold into slavery (see Matt 18:23-35).

Some would have said that they should pay nothing to Caesar because everything belongs to God (Lev 25:23). Some would have opposed any collusion with Rome. There were those who harbored strong nationalist sentiments and fomented armed revolt against the occupying powers. Josephus tells of several first-century revolutionary leaders, including Judas the Galilean (Acts 5:37), who led unsuccessful tax revolts.

In asking Jesus to take a stand on this thorny question, the Pharisees hope to discredit him. If he supports paying the tax, then he would be seen as cooperating with the enemy, and his credibility as a prophet who preaches God's ways as opposed to Caesar's imperial ways is compromised. If he replies that the tax ought to not be paid, then he places himself at risk vis-à-vis the Romans.

Jesus finds a clever way through these two opposite choices: one should give the coins back to Caesar, since they belong to him. He then turns the focus toward "what belongs to God," which, for believers, is everything. Thus, Jesus relativizes the authority of the emperor, by emphasizing God's ultimate sovereignty over all. This clever answer leaves Jesus' opponents astounded. They have no response and they depart to await another opportunity to ensnare him.

In the gospel, Jesus' interlocutors are not asking a sincere question; they are intent on undoing him. Nonetheless, the text can be an aid for contemporary Christians who genuinely seek to discern how they will relate to a government that takes actions or enacts laws that they oppose on moral grounds.

Should one withhold paying taxes, for example, such as some Christians, like Raymond Hunthausen (former archbishop of Seattle, 1975–91), have done to express their opposition to the stockpiling of nuclear weapons? Should one refuse to pay federal income tax as a way to protest war, as Dorothy Day did? Or should one pay taxes, but diligently lobby, vote, and participate in nonviolent protests as ways to communicate an oppositional stance?

Jesus' single-mindedness about the reign of God and his cleverness in turning a verbal duel into an invitation to become more deeply centered on the Holy One can help us discern our responses in our day.

PRAYING WITH SCRIPTURE

1. What "things of Caesar" are presently at odds with "the things of God"?

2. Ask the Spirit to help you become ever more centered on "the things of God."

3. Ask Jesus to help you discern your response to governmental policies or laws that are at odds with the gospel.

LOVE SAYS IT ALL

Thirtieth Sunday in Ordinary Time

Readings: Exod 22:20-26; Ps 18:2-3, 3-4, 47, 51;
1 Thess 1:5c-10; Matt 22:34-40

"Teacher, which commandment in the law is the greatest?" (Matt 22:36)

When my students are working on a paper, I always ask if they can summarize their thesis in one sentence. Similarly, when students are preparing a homily, I ask if they can say in one phrase what they are trying to convey. If they cannot do this, they still have much work to do to clarify what they are thinking and what it is they want people to take away from their paper or their preaching.

In today's gospel, the Pharisees ask Jesus which commandment in the law is the greatest. This episode is the third in a string of four controversy stories in Matthew 22, in which the religious leaders are trying to trap Jesus. This is different from the accounts in Mark 12:28-34 and Luke 10:25-28, where the questioner is sincere and receives affirmation from Jesus.

In Matthew's account, the Pharisees' question tests Jesus in two ways. First, all the commandments are important and all must be kept. If Jesus were to say that some could be disregarded, they would have caught him. More likely, the Pharisees were trying to see if Jesus could match other famous teachers of the time who could summarize the law. Rabbi Hillel, for example, summed up the commandments thus: "What is hateful to you do not do to your neighbor" (*b. Šabb.* 31a). In the Sermon on the Mount, Jesus made a similar statement: "In everything do to others as you would have them do to you; for this is the law and the prophets" (Matt 7:12). Now Jesus elaborates on that statement to bring into view the other side of the same coin: love of God.

The commandment to love God with one's whole heart, soul, and strength is found in Deuteronomy 6:4-9, the Shema, recited twice a day by Jews. The whole self is involved: the heart, considered the seat of emotions, the soul, the center of vitality and consciousness and strength or power. The command to love the neighbor is from the Holiness Code (Lev 19:18), which asserts that the way love of God is manifest is in love toward the neighbor. These are not really two separate commandments, then, but rather two faces of the same love.

What is not explicit in this text, but appears in many other places in Scripture, is that God's love is prior. Before one is able to demonstrate love of God and love of neighbor, God has taken the initiative in loving. When one has become open to God's free, unmerited, unbounded love, and has let the love sink deeply into one's being, that one then has the capacity to give love in return. When divine love overwhelms us, we are prone to ask with the psalmist, "What shall I return to the LORD for all his bounty to me?" (Ps 116:12, NRSV). The response is one simple word: love. It has two objects, which are inseparable: God and neighbor.

Today, with our rise in eco-justice consciousness, we would include all creation within our notion of "neighbor" to be loved. We would also include love of self, though this notion would have been foreign to people of the biblical world. They did not understand themselves in individualistic terms, but rather as enmeshed in a particular family, clan, and religious group, and dependent on others for their sense of self-identity.

When the greatest commandment is to love, it becomes very difficult to spell out how to keep it. Saint Augustine advised, "Love and do what you will" (*Sermon 7* on the First Epistle of John). When tested on his knowledge and fulfillment of the commandments, Jesus passes with an answer that cannot be bested, but it can be repeated.

PRAYING WITH SCRIPTURE

1. Take some time apart to be with God and open yourself to the divine love that fills you.

2. Ask Jesus to show you how to love God and neighbor most fully today.

3. When at prayer, breathe in the power of the Spirit to enable you to do what love asks.

WALKING THE TALK

Thirty-First Sunday in Ordinary Time

Readings: Mal 1:14b–2:2b, 8-10; Ps 131:1, 2, 3;
1 Thess 2:7b-9, 13; Matt 23:1-12

"For they preach but they do not practice" (Matt 23:3)

What to do when leaders do not practice what they preach? In today's gospel, Jesus addresses the crowds and his disciples, giving them directives for how to respond when they are faced with leaders who do not "walk the talk." He first urges respect for the office, "the chair of Moses," and advises that they sincerely take to heart what truthful teachers say. But when leaders act ostentatiously and revel in honor and privilege, Jesus tells his hearers not to imitate them. He emphasizes that all are brothers and sisters, with only one who is deserving of special titles and honor: God. He undercuts the conventional pyramidal models of authority and obedience by asserting that in a community of equal disciples of brothers and sisters there is no one who occupies the place of sole authoritative teacher, father, or master.

Unlike the teaching found in Colossians 3:18–4:1 and Ephesians 5:21–6:9, where the traditional household codes—in which husbands, fathers, and masters are set over wives, children, and slaves—are reinforced with Christian motivation, Jesus' teaching in today's gospel would undo such a structure. It is not a simple reversal that Jesus proclaims, by which the one at the bottom of the pyramid takes the place of the one at the top, but rather a circular structure in which all are brothers and sisters, equal in discipleship.

To create such a community, whoever has enjoyed exalted positions of privilege would need to humbly relinquish such status markers, and those who have been humiliated through structural injustice would be lifted up to their rightful equal place at the table.

116

In such a community, greatness is evident through service to the whole. In the second reading, Paul gives us an image of how that can be. He tells the Thessalonians that he has been like a nursing mother with them, putting the care and feeding of those who have been entrusted to his care uppermost in his concerns.

Moreover, just as a nursing mother surrenders her very self to her child, so Paul gives his very self in proclaiming the gospel—an exemplary leader who "walks the talk." In addition, he works so as not to be a burden to any of them.

The contrast is great between this approach and that of the leaders who tie up heavy burdens and lay them on other peoples' shoulders. In another part of the gospel, Jesus speaks about the lightness of his burden for those who will take his teaching upon their shoulders. He is intent on lifting heavy burdens from those who are weighed down, and taking those upon himself instead (Matt 11:28-30). And like Paul, Jesus also speaks of his leadership as being like that of a mother bird who wants to keep her brood safely enfolded in her wings (Matt 23:37).

In Jesus' community of disciples, there is no room for ostentatious displays of piety. Devout Jews wear phylacteries (leather boxes containing the parchment texts of Exod 13:1-16; Deut 6:4-9 and 11:13-22, which are strapped to the forehead and arm during morning prayer) as a reminder to observe all of God's commands (see Num 15:38-39; Deut 22:12). They are not meant to impress others, but are tangible reminders to internalize and act on the commandments.

PRAYING WITH SCRIPTURE

1. Ask Jesus for the grace to more fully "walk the talk."

2. Ask the Spirit to guide you and your faith community in creating structures in which all are equally sister and brother, led by servant leaders.

3. Pray with the image of a nursing mother or a sheltering maternal bird as leader.

INEXHAUSTIBLE LIGHT

Thirty-Second Sunday in Ordinary Time

Readings: Wis 6:12-16; Ps 63:2, 3-4, 5-6, 7-8;
1 Thess 4:13-18; Matt 25:1-13

"[T]hose who were ready went into the wedding feast" (Matt 25:10)

I'm the kind of person who is always prepared. When I travel, I pack extras of everything just in case I or someone I am with has a need. I readily identify with the wise virgins in today's gospel. But there is something deeply disturbing as the parable plays out. The women who come prepared for the long vigil won't share their oil with their needy sisters. Instead, they send them off on a foolhardy mission at midnight to go buy their own. How can such seemingly selfish hoarding be laudable?

Many biblical commentators would explain that parables are meant to make only one point, and selfishness versus sharing is not the point of this one. It is a parable about the end time, which speaks about how each person needs to be accountable for his or her own good deeds, or lack of them, at the time of judgment. Just as in the Sermon on the Mount, where Jesus says, "Let your light shine before others, so that they may see your good works and give glory to your Father" (Matt 5:16, NRSV), so in today's gospel, the oil that fuels the light is also to be understood as good deeds, and no one can share theirs with someone who has none.

Nonetheless, there is still a disturbing dynamic set up by the parable. It constructs a dichotomous world in which some are wise and some foolish, some are completely prepared and some not at all; some are welcomed into the feast and some are locked out. Matthew has a penchant for binary oppositions like this: weeds and wheat, sheep and goats, house built on rock and one built on sand, the wise and the foolish. But real life seems always to be somewhere in between: each of us a little bit foolish in our growth toward wisdom, all of us somewhat prepared, but never completely.

When placed in the context of the whole gospel, instead of inducing fear, the parable instead gives assurance that when we are responding all along to the lifelong courtship by the Bridegroom, we will be ready for the moment of consummation. We prepare for the critical moment of meeting the Beloved face-to-face with all our daily choices for living justly. Every time we resist hoarding oil for ourselves, not stockpiling so that others are left wanting, we allow Christ's light to fill us and spread to others.

It is as Isaac of Nineveh, a seventh-century Nestorian bishop, describes: "There is a love, like a small lamp, fed by oil, that goes out when the oil is ended; or like a rain-fed stream which goes dry when rain no longer feeds it. But there is a love, like a spring gushing from the earth, never to be exhausted" (*Early Fathers from the Philokalia*, quoted by John Shea in *The Spiritual Wisdom of the Gospels for Christian Preachers and Teachers, Year A* [Collegeville, MN: Liturgical Press, 2004], 315). Wise ones become one with the inexhaustible river of Christ's love; their oil is continuously replenished as it is consumed.

Being wise also means knowing that, as the first reading describes, it is not our efforts alone that make for the light: Wisdom herself, who is unfading resplendence, seeks us out. Long vigils through times of darkness end at the dawn with Holy Wisdom sitting right at one's own gate, wanting to be found. Moreover, a closed door is never the final act. Just as God's power burst through the stone door of the tomb, Holy Wisdom can daily open the door of our hearts, transforming our lack of oil into an inexhaustible river of light and love.

PRAYING WITH SCRIPTURE

1. How do you keep vigil for the arrival of the Beloved?

2. How is Holy Wisdom keeping vigil for you?

3. How do you keep the light of hope trimmed and burning?

UNMASKING GREED

Thirty-Third Sunday in Ordinary Time

Readings: Prov 31:10-13, 19-20, 30-31; Ps 128:1-2, 3, 4-5;
1 Thess 5:1-6; Matt 25:14-30

"Well done, my good and faithful servant" (Matt 25:21)

What can be done when one lives where the economic system is marked by deep inequity? One kind of response has been visible since September 2011 in the United States, as the protest movement "Occupy Wall Street" has voiced a broad-based frustration over how our financial system works. Today's parable offers another image of how an individual can take measures to undermine a system that allows the rich to become richer while the poor become poorer.

The story involves a very rich man who entrusts his possessions to his servants before going away on a journey. One receives five talents, another two, and the last receives one. A talent, *talenton* in Greek, is a monetary unit or a weight measurement. It is a very large sum of money. Unlike the master in Luke's version of this parable, who instructs his slaves to invest the money, the master in Matthew presumes his servants know how to increase his holdings in his absence. While he is away, two of the servants invest and double the money. For this they earn the master's praise and they are given increased responsibilities. The third buries the money, which does not increase the yield but was a good way to safeguard money and possessions in antiquity (see the parable of the buried treasure in Matt 13:44). For this he receives harsh words and severe punishment.

An important key to understanding the parable is to keep in mind that Jesus did not live in a capitalist system in which it is thought that wealth can be increased by investment. Instead, people had a notion of limited good: there is only so much wealth and any increase to one person takes away from another. A typical peasant would aim only to have enough to take care of his family. One who amassed large amounts for himself would be seen as greedy and wicked. In the parable, then, the third servant is the honorable one—only he has refused to cooperate in the system by which his master continues to accrue huge amounts of money while others go wanting.

The parable, then, can be a warning about the ease with which people can be co-opted by an unjust system, while also giving encouragement to disciples to take courageous measures to expose unfettered greed for the sin that it is. The last verse is sobering, depicting what can happen to those who blow the whistle on the rich and powerful. The parable also encourages disciples to find ways to stand together as they confront unjust systems and not to be found in a vulnerable solitary position as was the third servant.

Reading the parable from this perspective, one sees that the man going on a journey is not a figure for God, and the parable is not an exhortation for people to use their God-given talents to the full. While the latter is an important thing for Christians to do, it was not likely to be the way Jesus' first hearers understood the parable, since *talanton* does not have this metaphorical connotation in Greek. Moreover, there is an eschatological dimension to the parable that such an interpretation misses.

In the literary context of Matthew's Gospel, this is the third of three parables that stress the need for disciples to be faithful in the time between Jesus' departure and his coming again. In contrast to slaves, who live in servile fear of a greedy master who metes out cruel punishment to those who will not go along with his program for self-aggrandizement, Jesus' disciples live with trust in God, whose equitable love emboldens them to work for justice here and now while awaiting ultimate fulfillment.

PRAYING WITH SCRIPTURE

1. Ask Jesus to free you from any image of God that instills fear of punishment.

2. How is the Spirit emboldening you to counter systems in which the rich become richer and the poor become poorer?

3. How does your community of faith stand together to undermine systems that fuel greed?

THE SHEPHERD KING

The Solemnity of Christ the King

Readings: Ezek 34:11-12, 15-17; Ps 23:1-2, 2-3, 5-6;
1 Cor 15:20-26, 28; Matt 25:31-46

"[H]e will sit upon his glorious throne . . . as a shepherd" (Matt 25:31-32)

Classic works of art and literature like Michelangelo's Sistine Chapel and Dante's *Inferno* reflect an enduring fascination with the final judgment. Juxtaposed in vivid contrast are angels and devils, fire and clouds, the anguish of the damned and the joy of the redeemed. There's something satisfying in the thought that at the end time those who have done good will be rewarded and those who have not will be punished. To have a king who keeps an account of each one's actions and who then decrees who is blessed and who is cursed has appeal. This image is most satisfying, of course, to those who consider themselves upright and who suffer because of this, while observing that evildoers often prosper.

The image of an all-powerful, punishing divine king stands in strong contrast, however, to the image of God as shepherd in the first reading and the responsorial psalm. These depict God as personally tending the sheep, going after the lost ones, gathering them in from every place they have wandered, binding up the injured ones, healing the sick, and leading them to green places with plentiful food, restfulness, and refreshment—a very different approach to addressing those who miss the mark than fiery banishment. Many times in Matthew's Gospel as well, Jesus speaks of himself as shepherd and teaches his disciples how to be like him. He has compassion on the crowds when they are like sheep without a shepherd (Matt 9:36). He sends disciples to seek out the "lost sheep of the house of Israel" (10:6, NRSV) and urges them to leave ninety-nine sheep who are safe to seek out the one lost (18:10-14).

In today's gospel, Matthew holds in tension his eschatological theme that there is an end time when one's life choices become final and irreversible, while at the same time reprising his theme of Jesus as compassionate shepherd. Jesus is both an all-powerful monarch who sits upon a glorious throne and a loving shepherd. What stands out most vividly in Matthew's parable is not otherworldly visions of eternal glory or unrelenting damnation but the face of the hungry, thirsty, immigrant, naked, sick, and incarcerated Jesus. The fourfold repetition of this list underscores that Jesus is present and unavoidable at every turn, in those crying out to be shepherded. As often as Jesus' followers respond to these sisters and brothers in the way the Divine Shepherd did, he yet lives.

The shepherd's power over the sheep, as described in the Gospel of John, comes from intimate union (10:14), knowing each one by name (10:3), and an unsurpassable love that impels the shepherd to appoint his life wholly for the sheep, even to the point of death (10:11). This is power that is fueled by love, a shared and persuasive power, quite different from a monarch who is removed from the people, and who makes unilateral pronouncements. Today's parable warns not of a king who wields frightening power over unsuspecting subjects who did not realize their actions or omissions could damn them for all time, but of the deadly consequences if one ultimately rejects the shepherd's gracious beneficence. Such persons seal their own fate, choosing to be separated for all time from that empowering love.

PRAYING WITH SCRIPTURE

1. Ask the compassionate Divine Shepherd to help you relinquish the image of God as a stern, punishing king.

2. Let Jesus show you how to be a compassionate shepherd like himself.

3. How does your faith community work for systemic change to benefit those who are hungry, thirsty, immigrant, naked, sick, and incarcerated?

CPSIA information can be obtained
at www.ICGtesting.com
Printed in the USA
LVHW050146070723
751684LV00004B/241